It's a kids game

By Julianne Ramsey

GAME PLAN

Introduction

After the years my family spent playing travel baseball, I can see how easily it can be to forget that, at its core, baseball is a game of strategy, execution, errors, losers, winners, and game over.

When reading some of these chapters, I will get eye rolls or be judged as an oversensitive, overemotional mama bear whining about the whole youth baseball thing because her kids didn't make it. I want to let you know the real me before you keep going. First, my boys will make it in whatever capacity they choose, in this game and in any other aspect of their lives. I am 100% a proud mama bear. I do not whine. I do not believe my boys are better than yours. Yes, I am bitter about certain things that happened to us, and those things motivated me to write this book to help one parent, one coach, or one organization. I love baseball, know a lot about baseball, and I want all our boys and girls to fall in love with the greatest sport on Earth. And that responsibility lies with all of us grown-ups.. parents, caretakers, coaches, organizational leaders… all of us. Right now, the state of youth baseball, and, dare I say, youth sports as a whole, is wildly out of control. I like facts, I like stats, and I like real-life experience, all of which is how I wrote this book.

Both of our boys inspired me to write about this. Going on this journey together has opened our eyes and taught us enough to want to share with you. Nobody talks about the good, the bad, and the truth. I hope it helps you on your journey, whether just for information, changing your behaviors as a coach, parent, or organizational owner, or helping guide you to the right road to travel for you and your family.

Before we get into the nitty-gritty, I want to say that even though baseball is a game at its core, that by no means negates the skill, training, and hard work that these higher-level players do on an everyday basis to become better and more skilled at their craft.

Buckle up; the ride starts now.

First Inning:

The Basics

GAME:

"A FORM OF PLAY OR SPORT, ESPECIALLY A COMPETITIVE ONE, PLAYED ACCORDING TO RULES AND DECIDED BY SKILL, STRENGTH, OR LUCK. A COMPLETE EPISODE OR PERIOD OF PLAY ENDING IN A DEFINITE RESULT".

Oxford Dictionary

Baseball…. It means something different to everyone. To some, it's a way of life, thought of when we first wake up and our last thoughts at the end of the day. To some, playing with friends and family is a fun sport. To others, it's the most incredible show on earth to watch, follow, cheer, cry, and celebrate. To some, it means nothing. Poor folks, they don't know what they are missing. But for everyone except the last group, baseball is life. Baseball is fun to play and watch. Baseball is competitive and passionate, two of my faves. Baseball is a soul-crushing, heart-racing, hope-filled few hours of excitement. Even with all this, we must remember that it is a game at its core. Like with all games, there is always a winner and a loser. Our job as parents and caretakers is to teach our children to win and lose gracefully; it is part of their character and demonstrates their integrity. Remember: even when you start young, baseball is temporary; who you are as a person is forever.

Instead of picturing baseball in the next couple of sentences, please think of any other game or activity in which there is a winner. It could be another sport, such as dance, gymnastics, monopoly, chess, cribbage…well, you get it. There are die-hard players; there are naturally talented players. Some players have to have the best equipment; some get lessons to edge out competitors; and some only play because they're told they have to. Some players hate playing; others walk and talk about playing all day. There are players that everyone thinks are the best. Some players believe they are entitled to win based on who they know. I don't know about you, but there are a lot of different kinds of "players" out there, and navigating all those different types can be tricky. A coach has the tough job of navigating all those young boys and girls. Parents and caregivers also have a difficult job understanding their children and what is best for them. But, as with any game, winning is the goal. Everyone wants to win. After as many years as we have been through this whole lifestyle, winning means many different things to everyone.

All of this is to show that it's not just baseball; the stress, passion, hard work, balance, struggle, and frustration are everywhere, and most of this book applies to most sports and competitive groups alike. As you read more, ask yourself, "What kind of player do I have?"

Now, I want you to switch your thoughts to "teams." The ideal team is comprised of people who are all in the same category of "player." You will win a lot if you are lucky enough to have this. Unfortunately, that is not the case for most teams.

Most teams are going to have at least 1 or 2 entitled kids, 1 or 2 kids who are the "best," based on who knows what, 5 or 6 kids who love playing, always looking to get better by working hard, 2 or 3 kids that have little to no desire to be there or have a minimal investment in the team, and, finally, you will have 1or 2 that are just playing for fun. Yes, this is MY experience, but after being in the travel ball world over ten years now, trust me, it's pretty accurate. Does that mean that, with such mixed teams, we will never win? Absolutely not; we could have a tremendously great season based on coaches, parents, and organizational involvement, which we will discuss later. One thing is for certain: any team can win on any given day. The "worst" teams beat the "best" teams all the time.

Second Inning:

The Choice

CHOICE:

" THE ACT OF SELECTING OR MAKING A DECISION WHEN FACED WITH TWO OR MORE POSSIBILITIES"

OXFORD DICTIONARY

It should be their choice.

We all have been there or are here currently. You welcomed your precious child into your world and your family; they are perfect in every sense. You watch them grow, and you get to know what their strengths are as they get older. There comes a time when you think, what will be their "thing"? It makes my stomach ache to think about how young we feel we need to answer this question FOR them. Hell, we as parents are in our 20s, 30s, 40s, or older, and we are just figuring out what makes us truly happy. Some of us still don't know, but we think we can predict what a 2 or 3-year-old will want to participate in and excel at.

Wow. Read that again.

It's pretty unfair to them.

We are artists, so we will give them the tools to learn and love being artists. We will buy baby soccer balls, basketballs, and baseballs to see if we can see where their natural talent lies. We will take them on all our runs so they learn to love running. We will buy them a baby microphone so they can sing and encourage them to use it to foster a love of music. We make these decisions based on our wants, what we know the most about, and our passions.

It's natural.

Every single one of us has done it.

Multiple times.

Every single one of us.

It comes from a place of love and bonding, sharing our joys with our children, which feels fantastic. It is ok to do this stuff. It opens them up to many experiences that allow their world to grow. But just as important is watching and playing with our kids. If we play with our kids, they will show us what they feel good and confident with, what they crave to play with, and what they have no interest in. They will show us what they excel at (I say that lightly; we are talking about very young children), and they will naturally show us their strengths and weaknesses without pressure or judgment. It is what it is, and we can't let love for our things direct the next steps in their active lives.

Developmentally, it is okay to continue to do these things until they can clearly explain their thoughts and opinions with reasons to back up those beliefs. If they don't like to paint, play sports, sing, dance, play an instrument, ride horses, play paintball, go fishing, ski, run, etc.. Then we as parents have to respect that decision while at the same time providing new opportunities that may not be in our wheelhouse, but that continue to explore what makes our children the happiest and make them feel the most successful and confident.

That is what they deserve.

When I first met my husband, he asked my thoughts on kids and sports teams. Immediately, I answered they would play baseball/softball as much as they wanted. (See, I told you, we all do it) He did not like my answer. He wanted to make sure they would have enough time as they grew to learn more than just sports. I firmly confirmed that it would be no problem; they could do it all. With that confirmation, I had set myself up for high expectations and profound exhaustion. My advice… There is plenty of time to try different things they may love or hate. Yes, time flies faster than I ever thought possible, but you have plenty of time when it comes to this. No need to cram it all in between ages 4-9…

My husband and I 100% agreed that we would never force our children to do anything or play anything that they aren't interested in and/or that doesn't bring them joy. Trust me, to this day, when I think of them not playing baseball, it's an instant gut punch, but their happiness comes first regarding their likes, interests, and growth as young people.

When they were old enough to start participating in stuff, they could pick two things every "season." We played soccer, danced, played basketball, had instrument lessons, played disc golf, played baseball, played golf and more. We were happy as long as they were active Sept-Nov, Nov-Mar, and Mar-July. We gave them all their choices; they made the decisions and had to stick with them until that activity ended. This lasted until around 12; at that time, it went to 1 choice per "season."

We instilled this tradition below, which worked well for our boys and us as parents. Since they turned 12, we have sat and talked every year. What are you doing this year, and why?

Once **THEY** decide, we help them set **THEIR** goals.

NOT our goals.

Not where we think they should be, but rather where THEY want to be by the end of the year.

We write all of this down, and then after the particular season, we go over their sheets. Did you meet your goals? Did you like playing? Did you want to keep playing after the season was over? These conversations are not deep or long. These kids are young, and their higher brain functions don't allow them to give great insight. However, they can express how they feel and whether it makes them happy or not. This is not easy, and we made many mistakes in these conversations. But isn't our goal as parents to help our kids grow into the best versions of themselves? We certainly shouldn't aim to form them into better versions of ourselves.

Again, it's just not fair to them.

Now listen, I will not be winning any Parent of the Year awards anytime soon; I just passed along what we did as an example. There are undoubtedly many other ways to help our children become confident, booming, proud, and humble humans, which should always be the goal.

The weird ass reality

With that said, in all its rainbows and unicorns, the above way of thinking, it turns out, is in the incredible minority. How can that be possible? I ask myself the same question all the time. It's pretty sad, right? Most people think they know whether Sally will be on Team USA for gymnastics at 8 years old and that Joey is getting signed to the NBA out of high school, even though he's only 12. They know that Scotty will be the starting SS for the Red Sox in 2034, 10 years from now!

Huh?

It's astonishing the judgment placed on these boys and girls, and whether they will succeed before they have even reached puberty. How many amazing athletes were overlooked and ended up quitting based on these stereotypes? How many of these athletes peaked at 12? How many had the "star" role but couldn't care less? How many of these athletes quit because of too much pressure, lack of organizational support, or bad coaching?

WAY, WAY, TOO MANY is the answer.

Something is wrong with this picture. Haven't we lived long enough and witnessed many "GOATS" that did nothing outstanding before high school? Is it cool to hear a current major league player went to the Little League World Series when they were 12? Heck yeah, it is, but it certainly isn't required to be great, says the other 95% of major leaguers. As a New Englander, did we learn nothing when the 199th draft pick in the NFL draft became the GOAT simply because he was given an opportunity when another player got injured? Think of how many more GOATs could be if we let opportunity and performance lead the way. Instead, we continue with unfounded pre-judgment, word of mouth, and who you know.

Sad.

We think we know everything and are automatically given the right to judge children as young as 7, 8, or 9 years old.

Weird.

And it's not cool.

We think we know the magic secret to getting our kids ahead faster. We show them the error of our ways. We will prove that if we can do it again, we can make it this time, and we will demonstrate that through our children. It sounds a little whacky, right????

Again, it's not fair to them.

Are you catching this trend?

*It needs to stop, and it starts with **YOU**.*

ME.

All of US.

Third Inning:
Adults

NARCISSISM:

"is a self centered personality style characterized as having an excessive preoccupation with oneself and ones owns needs often at the expense of others"

Wikipedia

Regarding youth baseball and all forms of youth sport, **the adults are the #1 obstacle to successful outcomes.** This includes all the adults, parents, caregivers, coaches, program owners, and anyone else who assists our children in growing into the people they are becoming.

You played in college. We know.

Let me guess: when you played back in your day, you were the stud of the team. You would've gone to the next level except…. You played in high school and were the best on the team… You coached before and had the best teams….Did that offend you?

You're right. You did play in college. YOU played... why?? Did you play to get approval from your loved ones? Did you play to make other people happy? Did you play as best as possible, only to be critiqued all the way home? Did you work your hardest because other people told you to? I genuinely hope your answer to every single one of these is no. If not, please pass this book along to your loved ones.

I also hope that your answer to these was that you worked hard because you wanted to, because it would get you to your next goal. I hope you played to make yourself happy and undoubtedly proud. And I hope you had a support system that praised your hard work, cheered you on when that hard work was on display, and consistently pushed you to set bigger goals for yourself.

Listen, it starts in Little League… These parents and caregivers, at this level, are frieking awesome. Well, in the t-ball and coach pitch leagues, they are fantastic. Parents are willing to volunteer their time, energy, and patience with all the kids. Everyone is smiling and having fun. Little Joey is a stud, but he's running the wrong way. There is joy…and then minor league happens…or whatever it is called in your town or city. The boys are roughly 7-8 years old. Yup, that's right. The game changes when these kids are 7-8 years old. At 7/8, these kids are judged, manipulated, lose confidence, and lose the fun of playing a game of baseball. It is now stressful, at 7/8 years old! At 8, some kids are strolling onto the field with their $400 bats, $300 gloves, bat bags, ankle guards, elbow guards, all the newest garb, at 8. Some other kids are borrowing helmets, gloves, and bats. Some kids show up in jeans or sweatpants and can never find their hats or jerseys. Yet based on these simple pretentious things, judgment is again made on who will be best.

Incredible right?

Before proceeding, I'm going to use some of my Occupational Therapy knowledge to point out a few things about 7 and 8-year-old boys and girls and 30-odd-year-old adults.

Middle Childhood: Ages 6-8

*Kids are getting more independent away from caregivers

*Peer acceptance becomes more important. They are learning to

cooperate and share

*Parents should explore and allow children to make their own

choices when it comes to toys, sports, and other

recreational activities

* Kids develop skills and attention spans, understand teamwork,

and start playing organized sports.

* Kids get increasingly better at describing what has happened,

what they feel, and what they think.

* Lying, cheating, and stealing are to be expected somewhat in

these years. Kids are figuring out where they fit, the

difference between right and wrong, and what's acceptable.

You can reread those if you have to. Then think about your and your coach's expectations at 7 or 8 years old. The two are not the same—not even close.

Adulthood

The thirties are a decade of establishing the status quo. For the majority, this means growing a family, having a steady job, having a car, having a home, allowing for more financial stability. Routines have become more of the norm, and it is time to enjoy the benefits of all the hard work done in the twenties. The thirties are a time when adults are more mature and seemingly have their act together.

Both of these developmental guidelines fit in perfect harmony. As parents in adulthood, we should be able to foster the positive developmental growth mentioned above with these young children. But we forget, we forget the stage they are in. It's the old cliche… our kids are growing up so much faster than we did. I couldn't agree more with this, but do you know what hasn't changed over the many decades?

Brain growth and development.

Yes, these kids are seeing things they shouldn't, speaking in inappropriate ways, and acting like they are 3 or 4 years older than they are. When it comes to brain development, that hasn't changed. Biology hasn't changed, and anatomy hasn't changed. Kids in this age bracket need strong leadership and firm boundaries, but also increased praise to guide them in a positive, confident direction when they are successful. This is also the age at which kids are just starting to understand the concept of teamwork. STARTING… and also testing the lines of getting into trouble. Both things are crucial to their human development, and kids are frequently being penalized literally for being developmentally appropriate. Again, the problem is that the adults taking on the coaching roles have already decided who is good or bad, who should play where, or who's the rotten egg. It's not about fostering these children's love for the game and keeping it fun and not competitive. It is solely about setting a precedent on who will be the best coach for 7-8-year-olds. Pretty selfish, I would say.

It's more than embarrassing.

So why is now the time that all those volunteers disappear when these kids need the joy and all-around positive energy that comes with learning the greatest game on earth? What is left are the guys who had the loudest voices and were undoubtedly going to be head coaches for the next however many years. Why are these guys' children always the best SS in baseball history and the best leadoff 2, 3, or 4 batters that would make Ted Williams look like an amateur?

I never understood why, at 6,7,8 years old, when some of these kids just mastered their left from right, we are ranking them and assigning positions… Johnny is a lefty; throw him over to 1st, and for the rest of little Johnny's life in baseball, he will always be a first baseman. Why do all the coaches know exactly which position is best for their child, and no other child can even remotely come close to their abilities? Yes, at 6, 7, and 8, it only gets worse and more pronounced as they age.

This was a huge wake-up call for me and our family. When my oldest made a 9U all-star team when he was 7, we witnessed our 1st real example of "what the fuck just happened." Between the arguing with umps, the parents upset with playing time, the off-field drama, etc, from that point forward, we vowed always to be the "learn and have fun team."

It's not the most popular team.

I digress…

To get back to the coaches becoming coaches topic… Anyone willing to donate their time and effort into coaching a team should be welcomed with open arms. A baseball resume is not required. This is about loving and experiencing this great game with our kids for our kids, not having the kids experience it with us for us.

When the call for coaches goes out… There are three responses…

    1) "No way, I know nothing about baseball."

    2) "Definitely, without a question"

    3) "Sure, if you need extra help, I will do what I can."

There are a few outcomes based on the number of dads who played in college and were awesome back in the day. Too many "definitelys" looks bad for all the average Joe baseball players out there. Let's face it: most leagues overflow with "definitelys."

My husband coached both the boys through Little League, sometimes as the head coach and sometimes as the assistant, but all with the same mentality: we are going to learn the game of baseball, and we are going to have fun. They may have only won 1 or 2 championships along the way… which were terrific, but they all had fun, played many different positions, and sometimes sat out. I love it when my husband gets compliments to this day for the way he always treated all the boys. That's what it's all about… The boys… This became such a tagline joke in our town..”It's about the kids.”

Can you hear the chuckle??

"FEATURING TEAMS OF PLAYERS FROM THE COMMUNITY PLAYING AGAINST EACH OTHER WITH THE INTENT OF GIVING ALL CHILDREN A FUN COMPETITIVE ENVIRONMENT TO LEARN AND PLAY BASEBALL, WHERE TALENT IS LESS EMPHASIZED"

Wikipedia

This is a recreational Little League with abilities of all levels, where the love of the game begins. Yes, occasionally, there will be a team like no other in their age group, and those teams are entertaining to watch! The problem comes as the coaches are too busy trying to create teams like that, unknowingly destroying the love of the game for so many of these boys at such an early age. Imagine if Little League was just fun all the way through 12 years old. Could you imagine the positive energy that would bring to the teams, to the sport? Little League would be something to be celebrated instead of a source of aggravation and frustration for most kids and parents who don't have a relative or friend coaching/ guiding the team. That same coach is responsible for the judgment, reputation, and potential of those kids. Oooof.

It's true, and it's very real.

Now, I should interject myself here for a minute… There are GREAT Little League coaches out there. We were fortunate to have had some on our journey. Also, a giant shout-out to all the women out there who are getting involved with their sons' teams. We are amazing, and we belong there!

Some coaches do it because they love baseball and want to foster the love in these young kids. They want Little League to be a positive memory of their favorite coach because they learned a ton and had fun while learning. A memory of great friends who supported each other. In our small town's Little League, we had a few fantastic coaches and directors. All of them coached because their children wanted to play; it was their children's dream that they wanted to be a part of, not in control of.

Big difference.

I'm a solutions kind of girl, and there has got to be a solution to this problem. I have friends whose husbands are those typical "dad coaches"; I hear their opinions, too. I can even understand their rationale sometimes. So what do we do? How do we truly make it about the kids? How do we stop the my kid is better than your kid mentality? How do we halt the I'm better than you mentality amongst the kids? How do we get our kids to root for each other instead of competing against each other? How do we handle our coaches? How do we hold any of them accountable? How does your kid get to play shortstop when his grown-up isn't on the coaching staff? How do we get even teams? How do we make everyone happy? Or should I say every child is happy and excited to attend practice and games? I understand that would be nearly impossible, but anything has got to be better than what's going on now.

I'm not naive. Obviously, we can't make everyone happy. There will be kids who just don't like baseball. There will be kids only there because their parents signed them up and are more interested in the grass, dirt, or socializing with friends. But just because they don't want to be there doesn't mean we can't do our best to ensure they have a good experience. Can you imagine how many fewer children would drop out of Little League if we could give them a good experience?

The solution is simple here; the grown-ups need to get their shit together and quickly. These younger ages are where all the craziness starts. It is our job as adults to stop this shit.

Stop the judgment.

Stop the entitlement.

Stop the bad attitudes.

Stop the favoritism.

Stop the my kid is better than yours.

Stop the I am better than you.

Stop the win-at-all-costs mentality.

It's time to recognize that volunteer effort is just the beginning of

these children's experiences with sports, coaching, teamwork,

camaraderie, sportsmanship, and so many more.

The Fourth Inning:

The Magical World of

Travel Baseball

"Also referred to as elite, club, select, premier, etc. Travel baseball is an organized form of baseball characterized by competitive play, and you guessed it - travel."

Baseball Parks of America

To travel or not to travel..it is a very important question.

For many people, travel ball is a solution. Trust me when I say it's a monster of a different breed. But it is an option for many people, including us.

Our decision to start travel ball was not about our boys being better than anyone else. It was a combination of their love of the game; they wanted to get better, and there is a cap to learning with Little League, especially if your dad isn't a coach. We went to a travel team to start them learning that this love of baseball is all theirs, and we are there to watch, support, cheer (as loudly as possible), and help in any way we can. We wanted unbiased, non-dad coaches who get to know our boys and capitalize on their strengths while constantly working on their weaknesses. It was our "next level".

So, what is Travel baseball?

There is so much jargon when it comes to travel baseball, club ball, AAU, Triple Crown Sports, United States Specialty Sports Association (USSSA), Tournament teams, national teams; other than minor differences, they all lie under the same principle —the same idea. When people refer to travel baseball teams, they typically describe them as teams full of higher-level athletes who play in competitive tournaments and leagues. They usually have a facility of their own. They pride themselves on their offerings, accomplishments, and experiences. There are some great established programs; there are thrown-together on a whim programs, and pretty much everything in between. I don't know the real answer here, but I am guessing that back when travel ball was starting up (I'm going to guess mid to late 90's), I believe it truly was for the players that excelled on their other teams; they worked hard and wanted to get better. I believe it was for the "good" kids to play some extra tournaments over the summer. It has morphed into something insane at this point. Many people think they can do it better and open up organizations everywhere.

Truth bomb: 13 and under, any kid can play travel ball.

Any kid.

The number of frieking amazing-sounding teams surrounding our area is very cool, but also a little disheartening. There are so many options, so many opinions about the various programs, so many rumors, so many judgmental rankings. I will go out on a huge limb and say that all baseball programs are fundamentally the same, besides a small fraction of mind-blowing teams and organizations. They are businesses looking to get your business. We live in Massachusetts, and travel teams are a dime a dozen. There are a handful of teams in the state that are, without a doubt, absolutely outstanding. Those teams are remarkable and, again, entertaining to watch. This is also an expectation of travel ball. If your kid makes the team your kid has something special.

Our vision of those special teams is what we are made to believe will be the team our children will be on at our respective programs.   Then the 1st outdoor practice or game happens, and you think to yourself…

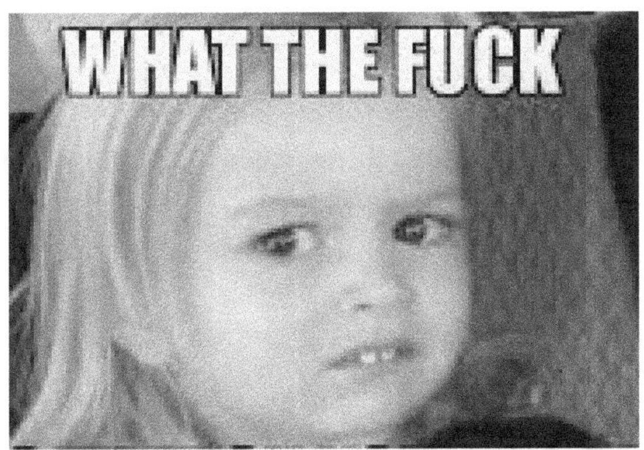

The 1st time you think to yourself, in the wise words of Inigo Montoya in The Princess Bride… "I do not think it means what you think it means." When trying to rationalize what just happened, all of a sudden, it becomes very clear this so-called "stud" team is a good team that will win games, but is very far from the team you were sold on. From that point on, depending on the type of parent you are, you will question all your decisions and all your conversations. You will keep all the promises made to you at the forefront of your mind, but wait; you are not allowed to say anything, or the infamous"that parent" label will be yours forever. Listen, it does not matter if you are the obnoxious, demanding, entitled parent or the level-headed, reality-based parent with legitimate questions or issues. You will be labeled as "that parent," but there will be much more on that topic later. Some of these program owners' entitlement is out of control.

How are we all still supporting this behavior?

It's absurd.

Again, I realize it all sounds so cynical. But as an ordinary parent who didn't "know" anyone in any program, and a parent of two boys with great talent and passion for baseball, these programs are tricky to navigate. Think 80s and 90s slimy car salesmen.

Here's my fantasy of the perfect baseball club…

Walk in to try out and meet many great athletes who are doing the same. As a parent, I wait till it's over with knots in my stomach. I have confidence in him, but does he have it in himself? When he is done, we discuss how it went and await an answer. We get the invite to join the team. The organization is proud of my son and every boy who made the cut. There is a practice squad for the kids who didn't make it, so they can work hard and become better baseball players. As training goes on, which consists of weight training, cardio training, agility training, baseball skill training, etc., the parents are regularly informed of performance, strengths, weaknesses, things to work on at home, etc. Coaches communicate with the whole team, setting firm, held-accountable expectations. We didn't "pay to play". We paid to become better baseball players with a foundation of good character. We paid for and received qualified, experienced coaching. We had a team that bonded so well together. Everyone on the team knew their role, supported one another, lifted each other up when needed, and celebrated their victories together. We may not have had an undefeated season, but we had the best season.

No drama.

Doesn't that all sound amazing!!

It is precisely what every single program "offers/promises." All baseball organizations know the fantasy described above. They know that's what we want for our kids. They know that their interpretation of our parental fantasy is very different than ours, and they sell it to us anyway.

Many programs are based on the various personalities and mentalities that exist everywhere. Every new program has something "better" than the last.

One thing I can say for sure is that there is a program out there for you—one that matches your child's personality, goals, and vision. It does exist, and you will be thrilled once you find it.

In our area, we are challenged by many cold-weather months, and unless we travel, we are limited to about six months of baseball weather, if we are lucky. In Texas, Florida, California, and all the other hot-weather states, there are 365 days of baseball to be played.

What a dream…

This directly affects many aspects of players and teams. Southern teams will have played 50-60 games before we even start playing that season. A 12-year-old who has been playing since T-ball in Dallas, Texas, will, without a doubt, be more experienced, knowledgeable, and advanced than a similar 12-year-old playing the same number of years in the Northeast.

This makes the location of residency a considerable variable. Up here in the New England states, most programs follow similar schedules for winter workouts, team workouts, lessons, etc, all to start the season sometime in late March, depending on how snowy the winter was, and ending in August. That's what we pay for… after that, you're on your own until maybe fall ball if your facility has that. That season can be very short, roughly September and October, so some organizations will play a schedule of weekend games, while others will use it as a time to train outdoors. There are always other opportunities to play outside of your organization…national teams, showcases, guest players for various tournaments, and, in some regions, Legion baseball or Senior Ruth. The best way to get involved in those additional opportunities is to talk to people who have done it before and who have been in your situation. Google is also your friend when looking to get more involved.

Those lovely, warmer states have far more options.

TYPES OF TEAMS

When choosing a team type, there are a few avenues. Speaking from the Northeast perspective, it's all I know. There are three different ways to compete. AAU (Amateur Athletic Union), NB Select League, formerly known as The Elite Baseball League, and Tournament play. AAU and NB Select schedule league play as the bulk of their season, with a couple of tournaments thrown in. And, if it wasn't obvious, Tournament organizations strictly play in tournaments. Lol. Once you reach 13, you will find that that age level tends to lean towards tournaments only. You can't play in AAU and NB Select. They are two different leagues altogether. AAU is all over the nation, and most people, when they think travel ball, think AAU, but more regional leagues are popping up all over. For example, NB Select is strictly the Northeast. I'm sure hundreds of other regional leagues are the alternative to AAU if you want League play.

Which is better: league play or tournament play? My answer is whatever works best for your family. League play will involve games every weekend, most likely doubleheaders. You will know the exact schedule for the whole season before it starts. There are standings and leaderboards, playoffs and championships, all-star games, and the whole nine yards. Tournament play will also be every weekend, and you will know which ones you are attending beforehand. Game days and times will always be at the last minute, with pool play announced only a few days in advance. You will know those pool-play games, but after that, it's a gamble that hinges on the team's performance. The really into-it dads are good at doing the math and the probability of all the scenarios in which your team will play and when. It's funny to listen to, though I am usually grateful to hear what they come up with to plan things better. Tournaments come in all kinds of formats as well. Some will have you play 2 or 3 pool-play games, and then, after the standings are made, run single or double elimination for everyone. Some have pool-play games to determine the top 4, who then play it out for the ship; the rest play consolation games. Some will be divided into two brackets after pool play: Gold and Silver. And honestly, there are probably a million other formats out there; these are just a few. There are a few week-long tournaments like Ripken and Cooperstown. I HIGHLY recommend going to one of those at some point; those are lifetime memories of tournaments.

Other things to consider when choosing an organization, whether for league or tournament play, include team size, coaching staff, parental involvement, preseason and in-season training, and the overall culture.

Team size

Team size will vary for many reasons. The teams for 12 and under are going to have roughly 12/13. Usually, you will see at least two teams at every age level until the big diamond at 13. This number may increase by a couple if you are on a tournament team, due to the need for more pitchers, given the potential for five or more games in a 3-day period. Now, I know they will promise you everything is equal and not leveled, but using your unbiased, grown-up intelligence, you know where they see your child fitting into the team. Sometimes, that reality does not feel good, but it does spark a different role as a parent; **being angry about it and blaming other kids is not the role to play**. To understand and accept, if your child is 11th, 12th, or 13th on the team, they will get minimal to no playing time. It sucks, but it is, unfortunately, the harsh truth about these very young players.

This age range, in my opinion, is when travel baseball is primarily a business rather than high-level training for high-level athletes, and I say that lightly… We are still talking about kids from ages 7-12. Be very afraid if someone calls their 7-year-old an elite athlete. Don't get me wrong; there are little spitfires out there who have natural athleticism and are passionate about baseball; we are just not going to call them high-level athletes… at 12 years old.

Here are a few of the problems. First, we are told these are the developmental stages of baseball, used to work on the fundamentals of the game, baseball IQ, and the development of good sportsmanship and strong character. Those sound great. This can be very frustrating because, as parents, we want our children to learn and grow. Still, the decision to play travel ball came with the expectation that the other kids on the team were like-minded in their determination, focus, and competitive nature… They, too, wanted the next level beyond Little League baseball. Unfortunately, this is just not true. Most of all, travel baseball organizations will 100% take your money, no matter what level of player your child is. They will have multiple teams at each age level: A, B, C, etc. They will swear up and down that they are not leveled. **They are 100% leveled.** They are leveling the kids at these young ages. And these boys and girls will never outlive this judgment placed upon them at 7, 8, 9, 10, 11, and 12. Johnny, the stud, is identified at 7 or 8, 9 or 10. It is so sad for Johnny, who, at such a young age, will now feel the pressure of being the star player on the team, always striving to meet the grown-ups' expectations. This sucks for Johnny. It's sad because no child that young knows how to be humble when all the grown-ups are worshiping them, and that directly affects their relationships with their teammates, which are vital for these young athletes. It's sad for the other kids who are of equal and, in some cases, better skills than Johnny, but will never get that acknowledgment, will never be able to surpass Johnny, no matter how much grit and work they put in; they will always be seen as just below the stud. So my advice is: if your child's interest and investment in baseball are there, don't let them be labeled the team's stud; at that age, that title is more for YOUR ego as a parent than theirs. I can not stress enough that the number of poor kids I have seen labeled as a stud at ten turns out to be your average-good baseball player, which is still great, but not so much for the kid.

As for the 13-and-over, we have learned that a team can have an astronomical number of players. For Example, our high school team carried 26 kids, a 15U team held 33, and a 16U team held 22. At this POINT, you must be in the best place for your child and family. You are paying a lot for travel baseball to be 1 of 33. You must understand that if your child fits in anything other than the top 11 or 12, they are never playing, except for being a PO or pitcher only. If that is the case, they will play occasionally. That is a lot of money to get frustrated and angry about playing time, especially when that time has already been determined by the historical hype around some kids. It's hard if your child is, say, "15th" on the team, and then you have to watch some other kids in the 1st-9th range not be the performers they were hyped up to be, over and over and over again. The hard truth, and it sucks. Once 15th, your child will always be 15th in your program. That doesn't mean that in a different program, a more appropriate program for your child, they could undoubtedly be in #1-9 slots on a roster.

I know this all sounds crazy, given all the factors that come with being 13-, 14-, and 15-year-old boys: the desire and passion change. Many boys who were in it to win it, all-out baseball, are now discovering other interests that require time, skill, and practice. The number of young men who were die-hard at 10, 11, or 12, and now, at 17 and 18, really couldn't care less is astounding. At 14, "studs" start to thin out, as well as some kids who were average at 12,13,14 are becoming unseen powerhouses as they go through puberty.

The unseen part is the part that stings.

Questions to ask yourself when choosing a program based on size. What is more important? Is it being on the top, most elite team but not getting much playing time, or playing on a team that is a small step down but playing all the time? It seems like an easy answer to me, but it is not for many. Being on the "best team" around is enough for many players. They are just happy to be on a winning team and be able to say. "I'm on ________" is what matters. You'll likely play with kids better than you, which is very valuable. Playing with those kids will surely help you become a better player. The problem is you won't get many opportunities to display that growth. Playing down on a B or C team can be great for your athlete. They will undoubtedly play far more, receive in-game feedback, have the opportunity to lead, and grow as athletes. The problem is that you are now dealing with a team full of kids, unsure where they belong. They struggle with the mental side of the situation, and too many kids see themselves as not good enough, which leads to diminished enthusiasm, passion, desire, and confidence.

My advice is to be truly honest with yourself as your athlete's parent. You know where they will thrive. For those under 13, I strongly recommend finding a program that will help your child grow. Championships are grand, but for those under 13, knowing proper mechanics and utilizing them during gameplay is more beneficial. It is essential to develop baseball IQ and the fundamentals at this age. Once your child reaches the over-13 level, he will be a better all-around athlete than he would be in a program that focuses only on wins and program notoriety. You didn't pay the money you paid to make the program look better; you spent your money on your athlete to become better every season.

Again, at the 13+ age and above, honesty about your athlete as a parent is essential. They should also give their input and goals; ultimately, those are the most important. Remember, this is their journey, not ours.

Try out at as many places as possible and get a feel for the environment, the coaching, and the other athletes. Go see the games for the programs you want to try out for. You will see the team dynamics and coaching behaviors unfold.

Coaching Staff and Parental Involvement

If you are entering the travel ball world and your athlete is 7-9, I can understand why parental involvement is important at that age. These kids are young and new to the world of travel, so having familiar faces could be beneficial. It *could* be because it largely depends on the type of parents who are willing to be involved.

After age 9, I strongly recommend no parental involvement. Again, this is your child's journey. Yes, you get to be a part of it, but you are not in control of any aspect. Your child needs to learn to be coached by people other than a parent, caretaker, or other family members. They need to know how to communicate and create relationships without your involvement. Support them, practice with them, cheer for them, make sure they are being treated respectfully, and then sit down and enjoy the game, the lesson, and the practice. That's it.

Off-season training

This one is directed to the colder, shorter-season states. I am sure there is good, high-quality off-season training in those beautiful, warm places; I just don't know much about them. Off-season training is essential; a good program will include that as part of its package. If you pay tuition and have to pay extra for necessary off-season training, you should consider switching programs. Off-season training should include strength training, cardio, situational baseball sessions, infield positional drills, bullpens, and hitting practice. Private lessons and focused groups are the exception, as they always incur an additional cost and should be worth the investment. Find a pitching coach, catching coach, and/or hitting coach with whom your child has a connection/ relationship with. A coach who will be invested in helping your child meet their goals. A coach who will stick with your child for the duration. If you plan to play for a program with off-season training, it is crucial to your child's success that you hold the program accountable for what it says it offers. It is very easy for them to call whatever they do "off-season training" when, in reality, it is not, and it does not help the team's growth and development. This topic is vital because programs can be deceptive about what they offer. My advice is that your child deserves the best, including off-season training. If that is not part of your tuition, I would keep looking.

In-season training

In-season training should be comprehensive and focused on building a strong, cohesive team. It is a vital component of success. Frequency and duration will change as your child reaches their next level, up to 12, big diamond, high school, etc. Your team should practice during the week during the season. Practice should not be just generalized drills that everyone participates in. There should be situational baseball practice (to boost that invaluable baseball IQ), position-focused training, drills based on previous game performance, bullpens, and live hitting.

In-season training also includes on-field training during the games. If kids struggle at the plate, coach them, help them with their swing, their timing… If kids struggle on the base paths, the coach should remind them of the dos and don'ts of base running. If kids are struggling on the field when making situational plays, struggling to track balls in the outfield, and/or keeping in front of the ball, coach them. Remind them of the whys of how certain things are done. Remind them of the importance of their role on the team, on the field, and at the plate. Coaches, please remember the age level you are working with and their developmental stage. For those under 12, there should be empathy and patience. The big diamond transition can be challenging for many kids. There is a vast learning opportunity at this age, which should be taken advantage of. Once in high school, you can communicate on a different level. Based on many years of learning, kids can be held to a higher standard. Coaches, this is a fantastic time; mutual respect, communication, trust, and transparency all lead to great success. If your program is not doing this, it is time to find one that does. Avoid the screaming coaches, the coaches who argue every call, and the coaches who punish mistakes. These coaches are not teaching your child anything except bad habits. Coaches whose #1 goal is to develop every player on their team are the ones to look for, hold onto, cherish, and grow together.

FIFTH INNING:

The Next Level

"Recruits need to show the strength, speed, and general athleticism to make the jump to college baseball. How serious a prospect takes the sport will separate the good from the great. Coaches are watching before the game, during the game and after to get a better understanding of the prospects character."

NCSA sports

Showcases, National team tournaments, Prospect Camps, and Recruiting

You may have already gotten emails "inviting" your child to an exclusive showcase, camp, or tournament. If not, you're lucky, lol. That part of the baseball world can be so confusing. Who does those? Are they real? Do they matter? There are a million opinions on this topic; honestly, I'm smack dab in the middle. Are they just money grabs? Are they worth the money? Will they get my child the proper exposure? Can anyone get "ranked" based on which events we attend?

Regarding Showcases/ Prospect Camps and National Tournaments, I would 1000% say you do not need to do these if your child is still playing on the smaller diamond. I understand there are some ridiculously talented and competitive 10,11, and 12-year-olds. In those instances, if your child is gifted and focused, and attending is one of their goals, attending one of these is a good idea if it will help them meet those goals. It will also give you an honest baseline of where your child stands. That information for future goal-making is very beneficial. The problem with these for 12 and under is their effect on the kids and their grown-ups' egos. Remember, there is a big difference between confidence and ego. And 12-year-olds have yet to learn of the difference. The qualifying judgment at such young ages is a gamble. A big one. Going to these at 12

and under will not make a difference in your player's future. It just isn't.
I promise you that.

As far as national tournaments, they are precisely what you think. They are very exciting. The talent is top-notch, and the gameplay is nothing short of impressive. You can attend as part of an established team or be a guest player for another team. If playing as a guest player, you give them all your information: age, height, weight, positions you've played, any stats you may have, organizations you've played for, etc. Then, you are placed on a team based on the info you gave them. After that, they play a standard tournament with various "scouts" watching gameplay. It is a format most top-level baseball players are familiar with and offers plenty of opportunities to showcase their strengths, given the multiple games. Scouts get to see their athleticism and their behavior between games. And when things aren't going your athletes' way, the scouts get to see how they react and rebound. Bonus: You will usually have to travel for these, and most of the time it's in a lovely, warm state. Yay.

Showcases are different. They focus on metrics: running speed, hitting exit velocity, pitching velocity, pitch types, catching skills, and pop times, vertical jumps, and more. After this, there may be a scrimmage to get a sense of in-game play, but not an actual tournament.

These metrics often yield a ranking for that organization. These rankings can help get noticed to a certain degree. Again, at the high school level, this is most pertinent. If you are a frequent flyer to any of these events, your name will surely get more noticed than if you go to one event when you're ten and then again when you're 14. Getting your name recognized = boatloads of cash. If rankings and visibility are essential to your athlete, then as long as you have the money and means to make it happen, go to as many as you choose and have fun.

A recruiting company advised that, when your child is a high school freshman and wants to play post-high school baseball, you should invest in one showcase a year to demonstrate growth and progress. Ideally, the same showcase should be used each time to yield more accurate year-to-year results. It will give a more precise description of the athlete's progress, strengths, and struggles. These numbers will be priceless as they start to make and maintain a profile to share for recruiting.

Recruiting

We are relatively new to this process, and it isn't an obvious process. We bought a book and did lots of googling. I recommend learning what the recruiting process is all about. I will give a brief, simple rundown of what I know. NCSA (Next College Student Athlete) is the most popular recruiting organization. I'm sure there are many others out there as well. People are usually 50/50 split on this, including our family. When our oldest son turned 14, we got a call from these guys. They were beneficial, but the sheer amount of information was overwhelming. We signed up mainly because we were utterly blind to this process and wanted to help our boys the best we could. They provided us with a wealth of helpful tools, timelines, and resources. They were very willing to chat literally at any time. A year later, we signed up our other son as well. These guys have an excellent reputation and an invaluable database of coaches and programs. It is a lot of $$$, but it's a great way to stay on track and follow a proven timeline. We joined when the boys were in 8th grade; if we were to do it again, I would say to wait until the sophomore season before deciding to join. It is a lot of money, and again, some kids who were dead set on playing at the college level in 7th and 8th grade are just not interested as they get older.

The other 50% of people also feel this is a waste of money. They want to figure it out on their own. They will write their own path to success, know enough people to ask questions, and have time and opportunity to open some doors for their athletes. If that works for you, go for it. There is also a big group of people who can't afford showcases, national tournaments, or recruiting assistance. They have high-level athletes who are just ordinary Joes. That is the hardest. That is where we were during this. Just ordinary people trying to figure out a process with many ins and loopholes that we will never be aware of. And the people who do know about them are certainly not sharing their info to put their child at risk of being overlooked in favor of adding equal or better talent who didn't go through all the hoopla to get to the point their child is at now.

It's competitive, but the truth is…

If your child wants to play college baseball, there is a spot for him on a roster.

I promise you that.

It may not be the starting SS for Vanderbilt as a freshman, but he will continue his baseball career beyond high school.

I am going to do some simple math on a small scale. A high school team that has, let's say, 25 kids on the team, and two go on to play college baseball. That by no means means that 23 kids tried their hardest and didn't make a team. This means that, through their baseball journeys, two decided to continue their careers, and the other 23 decided to end theirs. Now, could that number be higher if the athletes knew there was a way more than a teeny-tiny chance they'd make a team? Would they change their minds?? Who knows.

This means 8% will play at the next level from that high school. While that math is correct, it is taken out of context. It implies that 25 kids tried, and two succeeded. That is just not true. The two, wanting to continue their baseball career, will play college baseball. The other athletes see that, nationally, only 6% of high schoolers go on to play at the college level, and it is super discouraging. The part left out is that, unfortunately, at least 80% of the athletes who played in high school no longer have an interest, which is 100% okay. It sets the false standard of unattainability for most high school players. And the truth is that it is just wrong. If your child wants to play college baseball, they will. Most importantly, keep expectations and reality at the forefront; you will find the right spot for your athlete and family.

After you go through this process once, whether through a recruiter or on your own, you will have so much information on what worked and what didn't, what was necessary, and what was fluff. You will be a valuable resource for others. Take the opportunity to help others; there are plenty of teams for everyone.

I recommend familiarizing yourself with the NCAA guidelines as you go on this journey. Many rules must be followed, and there is a wealth of information on deadlines, the transfer portal, scholarships, and more. The NCAA rules also change, and those changes could affect your athlete and will definitely affect the recruiting process. The NCAA website is excellent, easy to navigate, and up-to-date on rule changes.

Here is a quick rundown of the College divisions. There are 5.

1) NCAA Division 1 (D1)

2) NCAA Division 2 (D2)

3) NCAA Division 3 (D3

4) NAIA

5) Junior College (JUCO)

The school division is based on the school population. Divisions 1 and 2 will be the higher-population schools, with the population decreasing from there. Also, athletic scholarships are only available at D1 or D2 schools.

As of 2025 there are 352 D1 schools, 313 D2 schools, 434 D3 schools

NAIA (National Association of Intercollegiate Athletics) NAIA schools are comparable to NCAA D3 schools. They do not have the

NCAA's restrictions regarding talking to future prospects. The NAIA also awards several athletic scholarships. There are roughly 180 NAIA baseball programs,

There are 189 Junior College D1 programs and 129 Junior College D2 programs. Both have 24 scholarships to award. The Junior College D1 scholarships cover tuition, registration fees, books, and housing, while the Junior College D2 scholarships cover only tuition.

In rough total, 1,597 college teams across all NCAA divisions, NAIA, and Junior colleges are looking for players. If your athletes' goal is to play at the college level, go for it; there is a spot for you somewhere. It will be hard, consistent work, but 100% achievable.

The Sixth Inning:
That Parent

"Sports Parents, Repeat after me... "My self-worth and personal reputation are not related to my child's athletic ability and performance."

Sports Dad Hub

"THAT PARENT"

Ahhhhh, these words give me fingernails-on-a-chalkboard vibes every time I hear them. I could go on for days about this topic. I stand firm that all the problems with youth sports are due to the adults. **All of the adults.** No discrimination here. However, being labeled "that parent" leads to much adult hostility and frustration. The inability to be heard, to be dismissed at every interaction, is uncomfortable and very frustrating. That parent… two words that create one label. One giant umbrella label. It encompasses everything, and every parent, including you, will be labeled "that parent" at some point. Justified or not, it does not matter. It is the reason program owners won't talk to you. It is the reason program owners talk bull shit as their 1st language. It's why programs, organizations, little leagues, and high school teams have zero accountability for their behavior and actions and zero interest in anything you say. I know it seems harsh, but the truth is, this is reality. It is a business for most of them.

Do you know what is even worse than that reality? When you do speak up, your label gets bigger. You are the whiny parent who doesn't get their way. You are the bully parent. You are the know-it-all parent. You are the toxic parent. You are the emotionally attached parent. You are the mama bear parent, the papa bear parent. You are the parent who yells at your kid. You are the parent who is never there for your kid. You are the over-anxious parent. You are the overly involved parent. You are the gossip parent. You are the drama-starter parent. You are the narcissistic parent.

There are lots of scenarios in which you are in great danger of being labeled that parent:

A simple question for clarification purposes = that parent

An inquiry in re: the coaching staff = that parent

A question about program development = that parent

Wanting to have a conversation about playing time = that parent

Questioning a decision made about your child = that parent

Wanting more information on anything to do with your child's team = that parent

Concerned with some shady shit happening on the team = that parent

Talking to the coach to get your kid ahead = that parent

You think your kid is better than everyone else = that parent

If you try to bully a coach = that parent

You try to bribe a coach = that parent

You have a conflict within the team and need help from the program = that parent

Holding a program accountable to what they "sold" you = that parent

The overall theme here is that you need to have a prior relationship with an owner to be given the benefit of the doubt. You are already "that parent" before introductions are made, before you even get your words out of your mouth. As a parent, it is incredibly frustrating. You pay a lot of money for an investment in your child and your family, and this is the treatment to be expected?? We pay thousands of dollars to have our child participate in their program. We have expectations based on their sales pitch. Isn't the customer service golden rule that the customer is always right? How in the world did that get flipped in youth sports? Can you even think of another business that would take thousands of your dollars, but the minute you want to ask a question or discuss anything, they are done with you? Can you think of any business that would survive and thrive like that? The answer is no, so why are we letting these people treat us, their customers, so poorly?

I mean, would it be absurd if:

> A coach actually played favorites that affected your child

> A coach acted inappropriately

> A program didn't follow through on its word

> A program puts its coaches and staff on a pedestal and downplays inappropriate behavior

> Coaches took bribes

> Coaches cave to parental pressure

> A coach, program owner, or organizational leader could be wrong, make a mistake, or misjudge people, but vehemently deny it all.

> But the fact is, all those things happen, and we are just supposed to shut up and deal with them.

> Know your role. Your parental role.

If I am being honest, owners and coaches automatically jump to a "that Parent" assumption because they don't know you. They don't know what kind of person you are, and quite honestly, they don't care. What they do know is that in the past, there have been some obnoxious parents who would make me not want to talk to anyone, either. I am not saying it's right; it was probably a good example of a few rotten apples spoiling the whole orchard of youth sports for everyone. I've been witness to a bad apple. It sucks. But just because that person was a douchebag does not mean I am a douchebag. You are judged by the company you keep, right? It turns out we don't get to choose our "company" in these programs, yet we're still judged as if we are the same.

The 7th Inning:

"That Coach"

"It's amazing the influence of a coach; A coach can build a spirit or break it down."
> quotes.com

"Young people need models, not critics."
> John Wooden

"That Coach"

Not nearly spoken of as frequently and loudly as it should be. Listen, I can't say it enough. I can't say it louder or more profoundly. **Most of the parents' issues are your fault.** You do have favorites. You may or may not coach your son, but if you do, you favor him. They will play where, when, and how much you want them to play. Regardless of their skill level and the skill level of other kids on the team. It's a fact, and nobody is fooling anyone. Oh, and it's incredibly annoying and infuriating. What happened to doing what's best for the team? What happened to being the hardest on your kid? I lived in that time in youth sports, and it sucked, but it also taught me way more. It taught me more in an extraordinary, life-skills kind of way. You learn early that nobody owns a spot. You learn to work hard and earn it. Your friends will appreciate your hard work when they know you are all on the same playing field. Literally.

Behave yourself when away at tournaments. You represent yourself, the program, our children, and the parents. You act like an asshole, and boom, the program's reputation is shit, as well as the reputations of the kids and their families. It is embarrassing. Stop screaming; stop belittling children in front of others. Stop being blatant in your favoritism; while you are busy doing that, a child is losing their belief in themself. A CHILD begins a new narrative within themselves, centered on "I'm not good enough." If you are coaching a team of 12, you invest in 12 players, not 2, 3, or 4. You signed up to coach a team, volunteer or not; your job is to coach the whole team and show improvement in every player. Good god, where is the accountability for that one? There are so many athletes who don't improve, and to me, that is unacceptable, especially if you are paying for travel ball. The advantage these coaches have is loyalty from their program owners. Whether the coach's behavior is appropriate or inappropriate, they will be defended to the ends of the Earth.

Man, what would it be like to have a person who would do that for us as parents? And they wonder why the parents get upset. Truthfully, we have experienced many coaches in our short baseball lives. A large majority should not be coaching. We have had amazing coaches, too. We have had the loud, hard-on-your-kids with the intention of making them better player-coaches. At the same time, they were loud and hard, they were also patient, knowledgeable, and qualified to teach and guide our children. (Kevin M, Gus D, Jarrod R, GD, Mike A, Willie T, DR, Mike D) We will always cherish these coaches. They are invaluable. Luckily, our final travel experience and program had very high standards for coaching, and it has made a huge difference.

On the other hand, we have had outrageous coaches. We had a coach who barely showed up. We had a coach who did absolutely nothing at practice, no guidance, direction, or teaching. We had a coach who came in and built strong relationships with the kids, only to leave after 1 season. We had a coach who still wanted to be playing themselves, so coaching young kids wasn't a good fit; it was a fun season, just not a productive one. He left after 1 year and went back to playing. We had coaches directly out of High School with no experience and no idea what to expect. I do not believe those young men were bad coaches, but they were brand new and never should've been placed in those roles. We have had coaches take money for playing time. We had coaches who told the kids to stop playing because none of them would make a high school team. We had coaches Uber to games because they had their license revoked for substance use. We had a coach who was abusing psych meds and had to quit just a few weeks into the season to get the help he needed. We have had coaches who got ejected for their behavior on multiple occasions. (There are maybe 1 or 2 reasons getting ejected would be ok) We had coaches give our kids lessons, then take the money and run. Gone. How is it that we, as parents, are supposed to keep our mouths shut and smile, yet these coaches can behave this way and get away with it every time? Not only that, but they also have the support of their program owner. Wild right? How in the fuck do we change this? It is absurd. Programs are getting thousands upon thousands of dollars to develop our kids, only to decrease confidence, diminish passion, and show no improvement. Instead of leading them to the diamond, they are leading them directly off the baseball field forever.

Not cool, coaches. Not cool.

The 8th Inning:

Lessons Learned, Advice to give

" Good advice is always certain to be ignored, but that's no reason not to give it."

Agatha Christie

This advice is mostly based on what we have learned the hard way, and the rest comes from watching and listening to those around me.

* #1 thing to say to your child before the game: work hard, have fun, and be a good teammate.

* #1 thing to say after the game: It was a good game. I loved watching and cheering for you.

*There will be a lot of different personalities; stay true to yourself.

* If you say anything, it will be repeated to someone. And it will most likely be different from what you said. Be careful with your words.

* **STOP** yelling at your child. Just stop. It is never justified.

* If your child looks at you after every swing or every play for your approval, they are playing for you and not themselves.

* Get to know the other parents. You are not better than any of them.

* Cheer for all the kids as loudly as you can.

* Stop coaching your kid from the stands. They have coaches in the dugout for that.

* Bring snacks and water to every game and extras for those who might not have any.

* Take pictures. Capture the moments. They are over in a flash.

* Realize you are watching your CHILD play their sport. Support them, cheer for them, enjoy them. This period in their lives is so minutely small and passing at the speed of light.

* Your stress should never travel downhill to your athlete. Do not talk trash about other kids and/or their families in front of your child. It's just shitty and will put your athlete in a bad position every time, and it will ignite the I'm better than you mentality.

* Be passionate. Be competitive. But also be a mature grown-up and know where the line between passionate and competitive ends and being an asshole begins.

* Coaches, take the time to get to know your players. The immediate judgments are outdated and unfair. The small can be powerful. The meek can be powerhouses. The big can be fast. The indecisive can be superstars.

* Coaches stop playing favorites. It's ridiculously obvious; it's totally disheartening and just shitty to do to kids.

* Parents stop bitching about the program, about the coaching, about the parents. Find a different program that suits you and your family better.

* Just because you start your baseball career with certain kids does not mean you all must stay together. You need to do what's best for your child, their goals, and their character.

* If you do separate from friends for different teams, remain a fan of those other athletes. Support them, cheer for them. They are kids and deserve your support.

* Parents, stop trying to "get ahead" of other athletes. Like you know the secret sauce but refuse to share it because a friend or a teammate might be better or do better. Absurd.

* Parents, there are millions of things to talk about during a game; please stop talking about other players. Just stop. It's uncomfortable to be around; it's neither kind nor respectful.

* Let your athlete talk about practice or games when he or she wants to, especially at the younger ages. Our boys are in high school now, and we have the "car" rule. We can talk about and say anything in the car after the game, the good and the bad. Once we are out of the car, it's in the past, and we focus on our next goal, our next game. It's not perfect, but when it works, it keeps many things in perspective.

* Celebrate the small wins. The big wins. And all the lessons learned in between.

* Coaches stop blaming the parents

* Parents, stop blaming the coaches

* Always communicate in writing. Lots of unfulfilled promises are verbally flying around out there.

* Practice with your athlete. Learn and grow together.

*Go to the games. I realize that with multiple children, busy schedules, and other factors, it can be hard, impossible at times. But if you can make it, even for an inning or two, go.

It matters. A lot.

* If you can't get to the game, check and see if there is a way to follow along, Game Changer being the most popular. Listen to the game; you will know what happened, and you can chat about it when your athlete returns. It will matter to him or her that you paid attention.

* If you can't follow along, ask a friend to take videos and send you updates. Again, it will show you are invested in their activity and that it matters to you. It will matter.

* Be genuinely kind and respectful to other parents, coaches, and owners.

* Don't brag. It's ugly.

* If playing doubleheaders, pack a lunch for your athlete and yourself.

* In high school, if the plan continues to be to play at the college level, invest in a nice camera and a fence mount. It is an invaluable investment to gain access to film to send to colleges when they reach the age you can. It will let you enjoy the game and deliver high-quality videos. To go along with this, remember to record it **without** the audio. Trust me. Lol

* On that same note, if you are sitting near where people are videoing or streaming, watch what you say. It will be on the video, and they will be able to hear and understand what is said.

* Game changer is also invaluable. The only rule is to shut your mouth if you are not volunteering to do it. The person doing it is doing their best. If you can do better,

volunteer. When I say **nobody** is paying attention to those stats, **nobody** is paying attention to those stats. Not coaches, not recruiters, not organizations. **Nobody**. If you are looking at the stats just for your knowledge to help your athlete, and you don't like the job the volunteer is doing, keep your own stats. Leave the game-changer volunteer alone for real.

* Have and/or go to as many team-building activities as possible, team dinners, etc.

* Volunteer when you have the opportunity.

* Remember when you shout from the stands, fence, or wherever at officials for miscalls or questionable calls. You are doing two things: embarrassing your child and making their current experience less fun.

* When being proactive for your athlete, keep a level head, present concrete information, and leave emotions at the door. Be a respectful adult your child will look up to, and not be embarrassed by.

* Behave yourselves when at away tournaments. Don't encourage your athlete to run wild. Don't encourage behavior you would not allow in your own home. Please shed the "boys will be boys" mentality and the frat-boy attitude.

* Parents, behave yourselves at tournaments. Drink and be merry, but don't be sloppy. Don't be that guy or girl. It is an away tournament, a little mini vacation—I get it. But there is no need to be the team or the coaches that others at the tournament are talking about because of the poor, drunk/ high behavior.

9th Inning:

Mental health

"To win at sports, you must beat your self-doubt"

Peaksports.com

I can't let this book go forward without talking about mental health in these kids when it comes to their sport. Almost 40% of kids between 12 and 18 meet the criteria for anxiety. At age 12, 5-8% of kids are diagnosed with anxiety; at age 18, that number blows up to over 35%. While genetics and brain chemistry contribute to those numbers, environmental factors are far more significant. Those include stress and stressful situations, family issues, academic pressures, performance anxiety with sports, social media, and so many more. We, as parents, must recognize this change in our children and help them through it. Help them talk to someone. Be a good listener and avoid judgment. Help them navigate this emotionally confusing time by supporting and lifting them up. Help them realize their invaluable worth. Remind them they are amazing human beings; everything after that is just extra. Coaches, get to know every single kid. Accept them for who they are, both in skill and personality. We are all different, yet we can all play together. Don't try to change who a child is at their core. We are meant to all coexist despite our differences. Once you, as coaches, accept that, your team will be much more successful. A great example is the 2004 Red Sox team; they were literally known as "The Idiots." They were all their authentic selves, embracing the starkly different personas of coaches and players. They were the absolute best team in baseball that year.

Parents and coaches, please let's take care of our kids' mental health. It is vital for the grown-ups they are to become that we provide the best opportunities and support to help them through this crazy, difficult time of growth between ages 8 and 18. As much as I could watch both of my boys play baseball until they are 80, we all know there will be a time they walk off that field forever, and then what? I would think success would be your #1 wish for them. Healthy mental health will go a long way in reaching that goal of success.

I often think about all the reasons that I love the sport of baseball. My list is long, but if you are also a baseball lover, your list is similar. Competition, passion, and skill level are required to play the most difficult sport. I love the rivals, I love the strategy, and I love the level of baseball IQ required to be successful. I love the history, the "greats," the controversial, all of it. Most of all, I love the fact that both of my boys chose baseball. They chose their passion, and nothing is more satisfying and soul-filling than watching them play. I have the fire in me to go crazy at most games. I have let it burn on low a few times. I have cried over the flames more than once, but mostly, I let it burn inside me and try to sit back and enjoy. Coaching from the bleachers is not our job, but it's fucking wicked hard to keep my mouth shut sometimes. I get it.

I want them to do their best and give 100% at every practice, scrimmage, and game. I want them to fight for every win. I want them to go through the ups and downs of baseball; it helps make them better young men. I want them to be good teammates and good leaders. I want to see joy on their faces, with the wins and the losses. The losses are a long learning process. Lol, Coaches, stop stealing the joy and start teaching them to steal bases. The loss of enthusiasm, happiness, and love for this incredible game is in our hands as adults. So, when you see a child lose interest, lose the joy, or consider quitting, what are you going to do? The fate of the choice is in your hands, coaches. The fate of that child is yours.

Do better.

Be better.

In the end,

"It's a kids' game"

Post Game Wrap Up:

Jacob and Nicholas' Stories

" Behind every great baseball player is a proud baseball mom

cheering louder than anyone"

Unknown

JAKES STORY

Jake is my youngest. At the time of this, he is 17 years old and a high school senior.

He started travel ball when he was 8. This kid, I tell you, knew his passion pretty fast. He saw his brother play, and he caught the competitive bug. The program we were in was good, the Worcester Tornadoes. Our older son played for them the year before, and it was a good experience, so we stayed. Because of his age, Jake played up on the 9U team. He falls into the weird category of his grade in school being the next age level in travel ball, but he would be playing with kids in his grade. Technically, he would be at the lower age level based on the age cutoff. This means he was 8 years old, and using the cutoff date, he should play 8u, but the 9u team is made up of all his actual classmates. We chose 9u; always play to be challenged, right? There was no other option in this program. He excelled on this team. He had a great coach. He worked hard. It was a fantastic 1st season. Coaching was clutch; he had a passionate, knowledgeable approach. He worked with all the kids and was respectful to all the parents. Year 2: Same team for the Tornadoes; again, happy with the same coach. Jake was growing as a player, for sure. Year 3: Worcester Tornadoes closes. The owner joined forces with another local club and hoped all the Tornadoes players would go there. We had looked at that program for our other son when he started, and the feedback they gave him at 8 years old was unfortunate and disheartening. Now, before you go and label me "that parent," and every parent thinks their kid is the best, let me tell you. I think the owners are nice people and are very knowledgeable about baseball… The thing is, you can't tell an 8-year-old that he is too heavy, and heavy kids go on the practice team.

8

8 years old.

Barely in 3rd grade. It was not cool, and it was not the mentality our family was looking to support. Now listen, if your child is 10-15 lbs overweight, and a total stranger sets him up for the rest of his baseball career with that level of belief in him or her, that is your choice. We let his skills prove his ability to be on any team. So yes, we could've returned to that facility and shown them what the heavy kid could do now, but we chose not to. But I digress. This is Jake's story. Another organization was planning to take over the former Tornadoes facility. This particular individual had previously run summer camps in the local towns. Jake attended one of those camps, and he loved it. The coaches were all young, previous college players, and enthusiastic. So when we heard that he was creating his own program, we were very hopeful. Both boys were on board with the change, hopeful it would be the "next level" step in their baseball journeys. So, here we were, Jake, on an 11u team. He had a good coach. No more dad coaches in this program, which is clutch in my mind. He got his 1st over the fence home run this year. He was really getting into catching, and the lessons he had paid off exponentially. He got better. Our only goal every year was that with our child's hard work and the expertise of the coaching staff, our child would improve every year. Year 4: We stayed, we had a new coach as there was only 1 team at this age level, 12u. We had seen this coach the year before and, as parents, were very impressed. We thought, damn, we are lucky to have this guy. And we were. He was young, passionate, smart, and good with the boys in many ways. He didn't tolerate bullshit behavior. He educated kids to help them learn more about their positions. He was hard on them, but with respect and good intentions. It was a good season. Jake was mostly catching full-time as the team's primary catcher. He was valued, and his confidence was growing. It was very awesome. Year 5: 13U... we learn a lot more about travel baseball. The big diamond must bring out the big guns with parents. Oooof. We started the season with two new coaches. The last coach had reasons for not being able to come back, despite many parents really pulling for him. So these two new coaches were very young. Extremely new to coaching and, in my opinion, thrown into the fire having a 13u team. It wasn't fair to them, and it wasn't fair to the boys. This was the 1st time Jake did not improve by being on that team. Again, we do not fault the coaches for their limited experience. Jake did get better through lessons and working hard himself, but no props fall to that year of coaches and staff. At one point during the season, parents took it upon themselves to offer compensation for our previous coach to return. Everyone was on board simply because the boys needed guidance. So, that coach finished out the season with them, and it was beyond a mediocre season. Year 6: Coach was back! He wasn't the same coach as he had been a few years before. He got angrier, more frustrated than anything else with the boys. It was a hard year. The coaching staff is telling the boys they won't even make their high school teams. Telling the boys he wouldn't take most of them back on future teams. It was rough to navigate. Trying to take the good out of each practice and game instead of focusing on the negative. That team was so talented. And remember, way back at the beginning, I talked about all the different types of players and having such a mix; how could that work and win ball games? I still don't know the answer to that because this group of boys was exactly that. All of them loved baseball. There was a wide range of skills, a wide range of entitlement, and sportsmanship. Some boys were positive all the time; some were negative all the time; and some couldn't care less if they were there at all. Yet somehow, someway, these boys won the 14U championship in our state and came in as runner-up for all of New England. I mean, it was crazy. It was so exciting for them; they earned it and celebrated it. The unfortunate undertone to that team was that there were a couple of small groups of boys who really weren't nice. Not supportive teammates… Not the "family" everyone talks about when referring to their teams. It was truly unfortunate because if they had all been good teammates, literally nothing could've stopped this team. Jake was typically the smallest and youngest on this team, but he never thought that would be an issue with "the boys." However, after this season ended and we were chatting, I learned about so many things I had been oblivious to. I was totally blind to how rude and disrespectful some of the boys had been toward him and many others. I was oblivious that a player's dad had literally paid the coach to ensure his kid played. I am still not over that… I can't figure out what is worse: the parent having the balls to do it or the coach accepting it. And no, that young man is not playing baseball anymore. I learned how many different parents had issues with each other. I was completely clueless. Listen, you won't see me hanging with a big group for a few reasons, one being my mouth; the filter is always off, and nobody else needs to hear that. Also, I'm always a little anxious and can't sit still, which has led me to take pictures and videos of the boys. That helped with the mouth thing, too. LOL, but it kept me busy, and I got some pretty cool shots over the years. This was all very crazy to find out at the end of such a successful season.

Again, I must include these disclaimers with every topic, lol. But yes, there are some absolutely incredible parents. I am still friends with parents from year 1, and we don't even play together anymore. The good ones are great, the shitty ones are shitty, and unfortunately, most often have the loudest voices.

Year 6: Wow. Buckle up for this one. OK, so everyone has to try out every year for this program we have been in. It's weird, but it's fine. As tryouts approached, we requested an "end of year" wrap-up from the previous season with the program's owner. He called us while we were away in Maine. He had good things to say about Jake and his team. We also let him know some of the things we discovered at the season's end, which he apparently already knew. As the call was finishing up, Jake was told not to bother coming to tryouts, that he had seen him at the championship games, and that he was all set. Keeping that team together was a priority, and that included Jake, " a stud." Jake then said Oh no, I will be at tryouts. If everyone else is trying out, then he would be there. So I took him to the tryout. He did awesome. We got an email that he made the "B" team. He and a handful of others were moved to a new team. This was mind-blowing. First, let me say that if my son is not good enough for the A team, then he's not good enough. That's one thing. But 3 days ago, we were told he was all set, and they were keeping the team together, and now he's not good enough.

That didn't sit right with me. We immediately get on the phone with the program owner. We get told that Jake's previous assistant coach was going to be the head coach, and he didn't want Jake. Jake then calls his assistant coach, and that young man gives a 14-year-old boy the worst answer. "I don't know what he's talking about, Jake; I have no control over rosters. There's nothing I can do for you." And hung up. Back to the owner. Now he tells us that his absolute stud of the program (not Jake, but from Jake's previous years' team) is looking around at another program, and he needs to keep this young man in the program. He tells us that this young man said the only way he would return is to have his own catcher from my high school team as his catcher. The program owner says ok. And Jake is off the roster. Wow. Jake wrote the owner letters asking why he was doing this. Why am I all of a sudden not good enough? His response was just him being unaccountable. He did nothing wrong. He put Jake "where it was best to put Jake." Not true. Just BS. Jake then called his head coach. Honest and genuine, the one coach for the previous 4 years always had Jake's back. The one Jake looked up to the most. The only literal reason we stayed in this program as long as we did. Again, this young man, whom my husband and I truly loved, was at his best when he was at his best.But he let us down. He took the money and, in turn, the friendship from that other parent, and we were no longer being fought for. So, Jake calls him, literally sobbing, trying to make sense of it all. Unfortunately, he gets even less of a response than the assistant gave. It was, "I don't know what to tell you, man". Wow. Gut punch. Again. So there were a lot of tears. There were a lot of questions… We were so loyal to them; how could they do that to me? I thought they valued me on their team. Why would they dump me and not care at all? These are his thoughts and feelings, not ours; remember, he is 13. There were a lot of whys, most of which neither my husband nor I could answer. He did belong on that team. He did make that team better. He was good enough. He was a great teammate. My heart broke into a million little pieces for him those days. It was awful. Knocked a confident, skilled 14U player to the ground. Took all the wind out of him. Remember when we talked about knowing your kid and letting them be in the driver's seat when it comes to their level of commitment and passion? Jake is one of those who live, breathe, work, and focus. He would play baseball anyway, anytime, anywhere he could, kind of player. It was Jake's choice, to stay and play on the new team, or re-evaluate his goals and try something new. He wrote the owner a well-thought-out letter declining the owner's offer to play in his program. The owner was surprised and tried to be upset with us. Oh no, no, dear, 1) It was 100% Jake's decision based on your information and your words. 2) You lied, disrespected, and threw us out. So, please check yourselves before getting angry at us. It truly was upsetting. We all cried a lot. We felt duped and dumb for believing anything they ever said to us. We questioned so much. We thought we were friends with the other parents, and to have them not want Jake as their son's catcher was heartbreaking. It all seemed unreal. Like, there was no way this could be real. It was an awful feeling as a parent to go through and to watch your 14-year-old child go through. Jake went to work. He looked up various programs. He decided to try out for an elite team. The reason being "they know what they are talking about." "They know how to work with high school-age kids that take baseball seriously." "They will help get me on the right path to play at the next level." All Jake's words, not mine. He did his research. No shit.. this next thing legit happened, I swear. Jake's catching coach texts him, saying, " I was just talking to so and so, and they want you to try out for their program. They want you to catch for them." Mic drops… it was for the program he had been researching. He went to that tryout scared out of his mind, but pulled it together like a champ. He made it. He made it onto an elite team at a notable program. More tears. He was so proud of himself. He went to the practices… night and day, from the previous program. The season started. He was the new guy. We were the new parents. I literally could cry just writing this. Jake was on a team full of Jakes. It was crazy. These boys supported each other. They were a great mix. They were great ball players, great young men, and they were all so passionate and focused. It was a dream. Coaching was experienced, knowledgeable, and approachable. We met some great parents. They were fun, inclusive, and knowledgeable. There was value around every corner, literally. They had a good season; they got some fantastic wins and tough losses, and in the end, they won the silver bracket elite championship. Wow. What a whirlwind. I say all of that with this little twinge, like, please don't let me get duped again. I kept telling myself, Juli, be smart, keep your eyes open, stay guarded. It must have worked because they asked Jake to return for the next season. These boys are all still friends; they get to play against each other in high school, and they are great sports with each other. We feel lucky. Jake did the work and research and made the decision, and it worked out. Who knows what his story will tell next, but at this point, we feel valued and very grateful he has the opportunities he has with this program. Year 7: Remain in the previous year's program. This was a big year for Jake. There was much higher competition, and it was awesome. There was also an additional catcher because they participate in at least 3-day tournaments every weekend. He traveled on a plane with his team and without us. They went to Georgia for the week and played some incredible baseball. It was watching those games on the live feed from Massachusetts that hit me; he is surrounded by the right people. People who value him. It felt great. They ended up playing well together. They didn't win a tournament, but they did tally more wins than losses. There were no complaints, and he was motivated to return the following year and close out his travel baseball career with this program..

Jake's story contains a lot more baseball than just travel ball. He played for the high school. He was a swing JV/V player as a freshman and did awesome! In his sophomore year, he was a full-time Varsity player and the 2nd catcher, since a senior also caught. He had a successful season; he caught well, batted well, and got more playing time as a sophomore than we ever thought would happen. He also has friends and coaches who he has valued very much over the years, and they invite Jake to play on various teams for random tournaments. Those are always the most fun. Our experience with Jake is very different than our experience with our other son. It is important to note that just because you have multiple children playing the same sport doesn't mean they are the same player. My boys are very different players and have very different goals. Jacob is very focused on playing after high school. He is motivated by that goal and prefers the route of travel ball, showcases, and higher-level tournaments that offer rankings and other stats. He wants all his at-bats videotaped to put together a portfolio to send to colleges. He also wants his catching to be videoed for the same reason. He wants it, and he wants to let people know about it. Jake is passionate and dedicated, and I can't wait to see where he ends up. I know it will be somewhere great, and I am so excited for him.

<h1 style="text-align:center"><u>JAKE STATS</u></h1>

*Stats based on the infamous Game Changer. Not all teams nor stats are on this list due to not using game changer at the time. There are many stats to choose from, but I decided to stick to the basics.

	# of plate appearances/batting average	Stolen bases/ success/ attempt	Fielding: Total Chances/% errors	# innings caught/ SB/ATT
10U Tornadoes	42/0.256	9/9	37/1.000	14 27/30
10U All stars	27/ .526	18/18	20/1.000	8 10/10
11U Energy	27/ .385	5/5	33/ .909	12 21/23
12U Allstars	27/ .292	6/6	12/ .950	1 0/0
12U Fall ball	24/ .600	9/9	23/ 1.000	10 5/5
12U Energy	81/ .493	19/20	144/ .965	81 46/49
13U Energy	82/ .345	13/16	172/ 1.000	144 82/102
Middle School (7th grade)	12/ .125	2/2	18/ 1.000	9 13/13
Top 100	7/ .500	3/3	1/ 1.000	2 1/2
Cooperstown	17/ .200	4/4	20/ .950	13 8/9
Middle School (8th grade)	26/ .397	6/6	33/ 1.000	13 25/29
Energy 14U	108/ .284	5/6	197/ .995	172 54/65
Shepherd Hill Varsity (9th grade)	7/ .571	1/1	16/ 1.000	9 0/0

NorthEast Baseball 14U	101/ .324	4/5	140/ .943	124.0/ 53/63
New Balance Select National Team 14U	22/ .267	1/1	29/ .931	29.1/ 10/15
Shepherd Hill Varsity (10th grade)	33/.394	1/1	65/1.00	42/ 4/5
Northeast Baseball 16U	39/ .401	1/1	78/1.00	53/ 11/13
Shepherd Hill Varsity (11th grade)	76/.375	0/0	135/1.00	130.1 33/46

Career stats based on the information we have. Could be a little better, could be a little worse, but we work with what we have.

Plate Appearances: 758   Batting average: .374.
Stolen bases: 107/113; .947%
Fielding Chances/ error percentage: 1,173/ .980%
And lastly he has caught 865.2 innings catching those runners 403/479 times!

Jake had an unbelievable summer with his travel team for the 2025 season. They attended many tournaments, which allowed him to display his skills, dedication, and passion. He attended many showcases and overall he played a ton of baseball. I can't update his stats for that season, simply because nobody was keeping them.

It was actually way less stressful. He was approached by several college coaches, and he had it narrowed to a few choices. He went on college visits and met 1-on-1 with the coaches. He met with the coach for the team he ultimately chose, and after that visit, he was very confident in his decision. This coach made him feel valued, that he would have a strong role on the team. He complimented Jake on his skills and all that he will bring to the team. Most importantly, as a freshman, he will be playing. That was so important in his decision-making. Proudly, I announce that Jake has accepted the offer to be the catcher and play college baseball for Anna Maria College in Rutland, MA. The moment he called the coach to accept was a memory that, as his mom, I will never forget. Filled with all the emotions, my heart could not be more full. Let's go, AmCats, defend the Den!

Committed
anna maria college   anna maria coll   anna maria college · paxton, ma
amcats · jake ramsey · c ·
jake ramsey · c · amcats · jake ramsey
ANNA MARIA

<u>NICKS STORY</u>

Nick is my oldest. At the time of writing this, he is 18. He started playing travel ball when he

was 9. Nick has been "playing" baseball since he could walk. He was one of those players you hear about who were just born with a baseball in their hand. He played t-ball and minor league, and it was clear he loved the sport and wasn't getting enough coaching at the recreational level. He wanted to learn more and get better. One of Nick's many extraordinary attributes is his ability to "know" the game. He is so smart in many ways, but he was in a league of his own on the baseball field. Enter the travel ball world. We were clueless, and there were about 7 million different opinions out there. We researched a few places. He wanted to try out at a place near home, where he knew a friend or 2, where there would be functional training in a gym, and where character was enforced just as much as skill. Year 1: First stop, Nick tried out. We were late to the game; who knew travel ball tryouts were the summer before the next season? That is a long ass time. Lol. So anyway, this program's feedback was that he undoubtedly had the skill to compete, but he was "heavy", so he could be on the practice team. Umm no. So much for that character component… especially to an 8/9-year-old. That is going to be a hard pass for the first program. We then went to the Worcester Tornadoes tryout. It went great!! We made the team, and it was very promising. It was an adjustment playing with a bunch of new kids, but Nick was lucky that in the 1st couple of years, he was able to play with some kids from our town, which made it a little easier. This team did come with some dad coaches, which was not what I had been hoping for, but it was fine. It was like we could step into the fire instead of being thrown in with this travel baseball world. The season was good; more of getting to know everyone and their abilities, and putting them in the right spots. Again, he was only 9; he and the other boys should have been learning all the positions, not just the ones they were preemptively placed. This would be one of the first lessons we learned and did not love. No matter the coach, no

matter the individual abilities, there is bias, and always will be.
There are perceived "athletes," and if you didn't fit that mold, you
were 2nd best at best. Nick's body type put him right into that spot,
2nd best at best, at 9 years old. Nick was the "slower" one. And so
Nick is going to play 1st, catch, and pitch. He wasn't the fastest
pitcher (at age 9), automatically placing him lower in the rankings.
The problem is that those rankings started at age 9, and there's
nothing you can do to change them. At 18, those same perceptions
and judgments remain. You can't work hard and prove them
wrong. You can't focus so hard that there is no choice but to
increase your value on the team. Your role was defined, end of
story. Sucked not only for Nick but for quite a few of his
teammates. Year 2: Same program. This was Jake's first year and
Nick's 2nd. Most of Nick's team returned; we were sold on the new
coach. He was a former catcher for the Puerto Rican national team.
He was smart, focused, and didn't put up with the crap from the
kids. He taught the kids, and the kids learned from him. Nick, as
you may note, has always been the kid who had to prove himself.

Literally every single year. It's just so dumb and unfair and based on the same stupid preconceived bias. But regardless, he has proved himself every single time. He worked hard and was a valuable asset to the team. The team itself was not overly amazing. They won many games, but more importantly, they grew as players, which is all we ever wanted. Oh, and Nick was selected as the "all-star" of the team and got to play in a game filled with other All-Stars from all over New England. He killed it; that was fun!

This season was also our first experience playing a tournament far away from home. We went to Sports at the Beach in Delaware. It did not disappoint. It was crazy there. We didn't have a chance of winning, but seeing the competition opened our eyes to the insanity of youth baseball. These boys were 10; we had played about 20 games that season, and the teams we played against had already played over 60 games. At 10. Wow. This is where perspective showed up. The New England teams will have a tough time competing against these year-round programs in the southern and western states. This is also where we learned our first parent lesson. We witnessed parents yelling at parents. Parents yelling at coaches around many people in the middle of the complex. My husband and I were mortified and embarrassed. This was not who we were or who we were raising our boys to be. This was the 1st time we had thought that maybe this travel world wasn't for us.

Year 3: Same program, we tried out again and made it back on the same team. We started the year with the same coach, which was the primary reason for returning. Nick got better last season, which was, again, our only goal, so we put a lot of faith in this coach. Turns out this coach got into an argument with the program director and quit. Ugh. Year 3 and year 3 with a new coach. The next coach was good. He was good with the boys as far as relating to them. He was not so great at stopping the assholery in the dugouts. I didn't understand it then, and I still don't understand it now, the way the boys treat each other. Neither of my boys responds well to it; it isn't how we talk to or treat each other in our home. I am not a follower of the "boys will be boys" BS.

Fuck that.

We have all evolved well past that saying and have the ability to raise our young boys and men to be respectful of each other. Doesn't seem that hard. Anyway. This season went well. They made it to the championship in their division but lost to a tough Maine team. We returned to Sports at the Beach again, with better expectations and results. At this point, we began to question our next steps. Nick did get better this year, but not as much as the year before, and now, who knows if this coach will stay? This was also the year, at age 11, when some kids felt like they were better than others. It was too bad; perspective says these boys are only 11; developing their sportsmanship and ability to be good teammates is far more of a priority than developing their ego that they are better than everyone else. It was an uneasy end to the season, with lots of talk of this one going to a different program and that one going to another different program. But all very secret. Why such a big secret? So nobody would go to those places and steal their kid's spot. I don't get it. Coaches from other programs were "recruiting"

kids. That is so crazy. Just because there are dads who have

conversations with other coaches does not mean that it indicates

recruitment. Yes, you may have had a pleasant conversation and

made the decision to try out for their program based on that

conversation, but that, in fact, does not equal recruitment. It is

deceptive and only intended to be intimidating and condescending.

When the other boys hear and spread the news, it's like so-and-so

had just been recruited to the Red Sox.

Simmer down, everyone.

Perspective people.

11-year-old boys.

So, during all this commotion and noise, we found out about our

program closing and the owner going to another program to

combine the two businesses. The problem is that the program he

was joining was the one that had no time for kids who were a bit

overweight. So, no can do there, would never happen, despite

really liking our previous owner. Year 4: I remember being nervous because both boys did their research and wanted to make a wise decision. I was nervous because I thought we would end up in 2 different programs, which ultimately would have been fine, whatever is best for each of them, but still. Turns out Nick was down for trying out for the new program that moved into the old Tornado space. We went for a tour with the owner. He had big plans, real big plans. It sounded amazing. Well, remember my version of a perfect travel ball program?? That is pretty much what he sold us …all the improvements… all the components of each age level…he made it sound like the Disney of travel baseball. So, of course, Nick wanted to play there. It was the new blood with big dreams and young men running the place. Nick decided to stay, but most of his old team went to other programs. Everyone just went their own way, and that was ok. Nick's new 12U team was pretty great. The boys were great, and he met some truly remarkable friends on this team with whom he remains friends to this day. The coach was the VP of the program. He was excellent. He was invested in the boys; there was some instruction during practice, and the boys gelled pretty well. They did pretty well during the season; this year, we didn't do sports at the beach; instead, we went to Cooperstown for the infamous week-long experience.

Cooperstown did not disappoint. Nick hit a home run that brought me to tears, and the whole experience, from the pin trading to the bunks to the free time fun to the absolute best baseball ever, was unforgettable. This year in baseball, Nick got better again in large part due to the quality of his coaching and his relationship with his coach. He valued him so much that he started taking his pitching and hitting lessons from him. Overall, it was a good 1st year for Nick. He won awards for his dedication and hard work. He had to prove himself again to this new coach at the beginning, but by the end, the slow kid with the nasty curve was able to shine. This was also the 1st time Nick experienced being pinch run for. This added to the judgment and lack of confidence in Nick as a runner. Nick isn't the fastest runner. He just is not. But beyond athletic in every single other category. He is immediately dismissed as someone who could help his team on the bases. From a program that prides itself on, "It's not about the winning, it's about the development at this age." Apparently, it's also about "well, we have to do what we have to do to win the game; we are competitive, you know." Ok, just me or those two entirely opposing frames of thought? I know it is also about destroying kids' confidence, pinch-running 12-year-olds in games that would not be defined by that baserunner. And please, I am aware of baseball strategy, and every run matters, and when I say there were times when he was pinch run for that were unnecessary, believe me, they were unnecessary. I'm not just some foolish mom who knows nothing about baseball strategy and is upset about her child. They were unnecessary. Whatever the rationale that was given to us was just BS, and unfortunately, this coach was not accountable for his actions. Do not get me wrong, I am very competitive and 100% on board with doing what has to be done to win games. I am also a very smart woman who knows there are many ways to win and lose baseball games. Pinch-running a great player speaks volumes and automatically shimmies that player down the ladder of value. And Nick literally could do absolutely nothing to change that. It disheartens me to think that if

five factors go into defining a "great player," and if you struggle

with just one of these factors, you are demoted in the minds of

many. There is a clear distinction between athleticism and speed.

Yes, they exist within each other, but you can have athleticism and

not be fast. This is Nick. Nick has athleticism that gets overlooked

due to his speed. Because of that, Nick is categorized as a good

pitcher, hitter, 1st baseman, and great teammate with a high

baseball IQ. He will, however, not be counted on or believed in in

a tight situation with the game on the line. That is absolutely

ludicrous. 12-years-old friends.12 years old.

Even though it was nice to have young coaches, they did not know

the age-appropriate guidelines for working with these boys. Brains

don't fully form until 25 years old. That means these coaches,

whose brains aren't fully formed, are coaching and making

decisions that affect children's confidence and love of the game.

Does not sound fair to the boys. My husband and I even set a time

to meet with the owner to try and talk to him about these types of issues. He was willing to meet and actually pulled off "interest" in what we were saying. He was grateful to have parents like us who speak "level-headed" and are "reality-based." Unfortunately, it was all BS to our faces. Nick was set up now in this program with a reputation and a label. He isn't athletic; he's not going to be the ace, and for every answer to every question we have about Nick, it will always be the same..Nick has to lose weight and get more athletic. I think the thing that surprises me the most is that all these people say the same thing. Do they think we don't know this about Nick? That we, as his parents, didn't do everything, and I mean everything, to help him meet their expectations. Do they think that Nick just ignored all their advice and said fuck it? There is no way, that is not the human being Nick is.

Year 5: Nick chose to return to this program, even with his label, and was determined to overcome that stupid stereotype. Honestly, it was more about the teammates and the friends. Nick continued to get lessons from last year's coach…This year, he went in with many questions, asking for help to work on his weaknesses. His lessons went well, but he never really progressed a ton. There wasn't a lot of feedback, homework, or push to work harder. The boys are 13 this year; the bigger the diamond, the more competition, the more serious and focused. This is what Nick has been waiting for. Lol. 5th year, you guessed it, another new coach. This one is one for the record books. He was an older gentleman who lasted, I think, 1 month before having to be hospitalized for his mental health. To this day, I think about him and hope he is doing well. We got the assistant coach, a much younger man. He liked and related to Nick because he was always the "bigger" one on his teams growing up. They had a great connection. Nick proved himself once again to be a very valuable asset. He was named Captain. We had a couple of new kids on the team this year, and they brought the team to a new level, which was great. We had an ok season. If we played .500 ball, we would be lucky. Nick was given the MVP of the team as well as the Roberto Clemente Award, which was all about character. We were so proud of him. He also had 8 complete games on the mound. It was not as competitive a year as we had hoped and were led to believe it would be. But Nick felt valued, and that was what was most important. Year 6: This year's outlook felt better. He asked himself if his coach could work with him to lose weight and get in good shape for the following season, and not be pinch run for. We said, if that is what you need to meet your goals, let's do it. During this time, I ran a gym out of our home in our garage. So we talked to the coach. He knew the goal…decrease weight and increase speed. He was happy to help, and I'm sure the cash was also motivating. So he came to our home and worked out with Nick in the gym 2-3x / week for 6 months. The money we spent. Oooof. But Nick and the coach were happy, and gains were being made. Towards the end of these workouts, Nick came to me saying he thought something was off with the coach and that he had hinted that Nick would not be starting at his previous position, where he earned MVP. So we told Nick to talk to him and ask him what was up. This is now the 14U team, so it's time for Nick to communicate for himself and take responsibility for his role. That coach told Nick that he had caved to parental pressures and that one of the new boys from last year would be starting at 1st. He told Nick this young man's parents had threatened to leave if he didn't play their son. So Nick was just out? That didn't make sense. He worked all winter on meeting his goals, but also the goals of the coach. So now comes opening day…Nick is benched. Games 2 and 3 benched. And I should be honest; he did pitch a couple of innings in one of those games, but that was it. It was devastating to him. All that time, all that hard work, all the talks of confidence. It was like a nightmare because it couldn't be real. Nick asked if he could meet with his coach, the program's owner, and his lessons coach. They resistantly agreed. They were under the impression that we had Nick speaking for us, as opposed to the truth, that it was all Nick; baseball was too important to him to let this continue. So the 6 of us sat in an office. Nick spoke his piece and expressed his concern about retaliation just for having the meeting. There was a banquet of bullshit going on in that office, but we weren't hungry for that crap… "We believe in you, Nick," "You are valuable to

us," "and there will be no retaliation." That was on a Wednesday.
The following weekend, we were to have a tournament for
Mother's Day. It was cold and rainy, but we were hopeful for a
good weekend of games after our meeting. Game 1: Nick benched.
Game 2: Pitched two innings. I pulled my hoodie as high as it
could go and pulled those strings so tight that I could sob and
nobody could see me. And I did. I sobbed. I lost it. I can't describe
what I felt in words, but that was the 1st time I did not enjoy even
1 minute of baseball. It was terrible. After those games and
walking back to our car, it was the 1st time I saw Nick's heartbreak
and anger come to light for others to see. He was done. Done being
disrespected, overlooked, dealing with people who were supposed
to be more mature than him, but clearly were not. He was right. He
didn't deserve any of this. He was the scapegoat. It was awful to
watch grown-ups do this to a 14-year-old child. But, despite the pit
in our stomachs, we stuck it out the best we could. He gave 100%
at each practice and each game. Most of his teammates supported
Nick and were pretty awesome to him. Those boys are the special

ones. Others jumped on board with the Nick isn't good enough bullshit. It was a very tough season; He still killed it with pitching and his hitting, and well, who knows about his running because he was still getting run for. So fucking dumb. The team became more divided as the season went on. Between the coach' disrespect, the parents that teamed up with the coach to divide the boys against each other to define the "good kids" group, and the shitty things being said by some boys to other boys is enough to make you sick. Again, I don't understand boy banter or whatever you want to call it, but I do know there is a line, and these particular boys crossed that line one too many times. It was deplorable. So, here comes the final what in the actual fuck of Nick's travel ball experience. We had one last tournament; it was in Hershey, PA. I'm pretty sure, and not to speak for anyone else, but I truly don't believe anyone wanted to be there. There was a weird vibe from the beginning. People weren't all hanging out together. The "good kids" group got a separate hotel and didn't want in on the team stuff. The other kids were just awkward; people knew some of the behind-the-scenes chit-chat, and some didn't. Some who were "loyal" were awkward towards others because they thought they knew information that was not flattering to some players. It was just an uncomfortable environment to be in. Nick was with his friends. They made the most of it. Nick appreciated them, and they were cool with Nick. Gameplay came, and I think you get the gist of how these games might have gone. lol. Anyway, we had to leave this tournament early because our other son had to be in Cooperstown on the same day as the last day of the tournament. It was pre-arranged since the beginning of the season, so it was no surprise to anyone. So we left in the 4th inning of the final consolation game. We arrived in Cooperstown, so happy for this week with Jake, and to be done with that other team for Nick. We had literally just settled into our room when my phone and Nick's phone started lighting up. It was a dear friend from Nick's team. She called me to tell me what had happened after we left and to get me the information before Nick heard it. Well, it was too late because, as she told me, Nick's friends were telling him. Buckle up. Apparently, after we left, a parent on our team decided to stand up and let everyone there know how he (they) felt about Nick. Let's see… Nick is a fat, lazy detriment to the team and doesn't deserve to be on the same team as his son. He can't even catch a fly ball. I'm sorry. What did you say? This is my mama bear reaction… You are a fuckin wimp.. wait til we leave to you make that proclamation. Your proclamation about another 14-year-old boy.

Wow.

All the parents heard it. All the kids heard it. I was in utter disbelief. Our only concern was Nick. How do we get him through this? After his history of being misjudged, disrespected, and crushed, how do we make him understand? Understand how so many adults have let him down by doing what he loves the most. Understand that this parent is full of shit, and the fact that he thinks it's okay to bully a 14-year-old is disturbing and ugly. However, those are his issues that need to be worked out. How do we tell Nick he is still a fantastic baseball player and make him know it's true? We did not know those answers; we gave him as much love as possible. His friends gave him their support. They knew it was wrong. Very wrong. We rallied around our family and our baseball family to get through it. It's over 4 years later, and I still don't know if we are all over it. I don't know if we ever will be. In that 1 moment, some jackass parent changed the trajectory of Nick's baseball life. Congratulations to him. Fucker. It just simply blows my mind that a parent would A- think that of a child and B- decide it would be ok to say it out loud and proud for everyone to hear. It's just too awful to wrap my brain around. It hurts my heart that the group those parents are in was the "good kids" group. Did they all feel the same way about a child? Did they all give each other high fives and nod their heads in a fuck yea kind of way when that asshole spewed his words? I'm afraid I don't know the answer to that question; I'm more afraid of knowing it to be true. So after we returned home, it wouldn't be long before tryouts for the following season. Before Nick would even begin to consider going back, we needed to chat with the owners. They had already heard what went down. How is that frieking possible..fucking people can not mind their own fucking business. In our meeting, we were told how "appalled" they were, how awful it was, and how bad they felt for Nick. They also said that that particular family would not be allowed back into the program based on this behavior. Side note: I do not believe that to be true; if that family went in tomorrow, that man would take their money in a heartbeat. Let it be noted that this family and three others (the "good kids") had already committed to another program for the following year. So the point was mute. But the team for the following year was hopeful. It is mainly filled with supportive, passionate, highly skilled players from the years before. The program owner tells us, "I will go to the tryouts, give an honest assessment, and we will meet again." We go to tryouts. Nick kills it. Again. So we go to his office. " Nick is 1 second slower than the fastest kid running to 1st. He is 3.5 seconds slower running from 1st to 3rd. He has less range at 1st base than other kids." He says out of "loyalty," he will give Nick a roster spot, but "don't expect to play." We responded that he was okay with sitting; every child should be OK with sitting, which is being a good teammate. His response: " No, I mean, he won't play at all." What in the actual fuck. Nick's choice, he composed a very nicely written declination of his offer letter. Give me a fucking break. The other kids are just faster, is bullshit.

Believe me, as a previous college softball athlete and Occupational Therapist by trade, my husband has his doctorate in Physical Therapy, as well as seven private clinics primarily focused on sports management; we are well aware of the need for athleticism. We know the importance of speed and agility. We know the benefits those things bring to a team. We also know it is one facet of many facets required to be an excellent athlete in the baseball world. It's a disservice to Nick that he gets eliminated from being seen as one of the best based on a 1-second difference on the base paths. We know Nick is bigger and slower, but what if his coaches worked with him to get him faster? What if even one coach legitimately believed in Nick and believed that with their help, Nick could outgrow such prejudice? How sad is it that not one coach, not one grown-up, showed Nick the respect of any of that?

Not one. So ridiculously sad. We know that Nick has weaknesses, which we will continue to work on. What we don't understand is what about all these amazing studs… they may be faster, but they are definitely lacking in way more facets than Nick. But somehow, someway, everyone can overlook 77 errors, a .100 batting average, and a shitty teammate attitude to allow those boys to remain the best of the best.

It truly is fucked up.

We took some time before talking to Nick about future baseball after all this. He needed to process; we needed to process, and we needed a not-so-hurt heart and not-so-angry mind. Year 7: Nick's decision.. No more travel ball. He decided he would work harder than ever; he lost every last pound of the 30 pounds that he was overweight. 30 pounds, people; he wasn't 100 pounds overweight, flopping around like a blob. He went to the gym almost every day. Running on the treadmill, doing sprints, and long runs. We took our travel ball money and hired a new pitching coach. He was out of Cressey Sports Performance, and I can say their name because they deserve to be noted. They took Nick in, and he worked with Jordan. By the time it came for high school tryouts, he was ready. Now listen, we have always told our boys, don't worry, once you get to high school, there will be no bias. It's a clean slate. You get to go out there and prove yourself. It's going to be amazing. Reality slap..that parent from the team that proclaimed his hatred for my child, yeah, his son goes to the same high school. So they will both be trying out. Lovely. No anxiety there at all. Lol. Then we find out there's a new coach for the high school team. Holy shit, I know him!! He grew up in my neighborhood; we played wiffle ball every summer in my and my neighbor's backyard. Ra Stadium… it was the best. So nuts! Is this finally the opportunity for us to "know" someone? The problem is we are so far from those people. Talking to him to get in on the inside track feels dirty. It feels disrespectful to the coach, sneaky, and sketchy. We decide, as we always have, to let Nick's abilities and skills show his capabilities. Unfortunately, and not surprisingly, others did not feel the same way. So, my telling my boys there was no bias and that the coach would be looking at all of you for the 1st time and making his own choices was bologna. The new coach already "knew" everything. He knew who the greats were and who the stars would be. So disappointing. Again. But he tried out and made JV. He excelled on JV, pitching, hitting, running, and 1st base/3rd base. He still wasn't the fastest, but he was in a pack with everyone else. 1st base was his; he killed it there, was skilled and smart, was strategic, knew all the dimensions of playing there, and had good range. His pitching was amazing. He had learned three new pitches, so he was up to 6 as a freshman and dominated. He was named team captain and worked hard to meet those expectations. He wasn't the highest-velocity pitcher, but he was the most accurate and diverse pitcher. His pitching was clutch, and he even had his first varsity pitching appearance, in which he killed it with a 1-2-3 inning with two strikeouts. My body could've burst with pride and happiness for him. I won't forget that moment ever. It happened; you could feel his confidence coming back. He was happy again playing baseball. As far as after high school season, he would now have nothing, and that was hard to handle. But he just said he wanted to keep grinding. He knew he had a few things to work on with hitting, so we worked with the coach in the off-season, and he was improving. Summer came, and I think he missed his travel team, friends, and the fun times. As his mom, I am proud of him. I believe he made the right decision. He propelled forward with maturity. He was grounded and hardworking. He reflected on that year and decided he wanted to start a business called Enjoyment Athletics. He would sell water bottles, cooling towels, and hats, all to spread the message of keeping sports fun. He wanted to remind people with every sip and swipe of the towel that they are playing a game and games are fun! The amount of success he had within our town and amongst family and friends was insane. I mean, really, can you believe this kid?? Talk about making lemonade. Good lord. So again, off-season workouts and lessons continue with 1 goal in mind… to make Varsity. This was also the summer when Nick was an assistant coach for the 14U team. He did a stellar job coaching, and as you read in Jake's story, Nick coached them to a state championship. Year 8: Nick was super nervous, but from my standpoint, he was ready. He was... he made Varsity... primary position pitcher, secondary 1st base. So exciting! It was sophomore year, and he was ready. The kid pitched like a rock star. I believe he was 5th in their division of all the sophomores! He pitched once a week, and in every game, except one, he came out with the lead. Very impressive for a sophomore on Varsity! Do I believe there was enough faith in Nick to finish out some games? No. Do I believe there was any faith in Nick to play 1st base? No. And, are we back where we started when it comes to him getting run for? Yes. But Nick is happy. He loves pitching. We absolutely love watching him pitch. I really and truly wish there wasn't so much "parental insight" given to the coach, and the coach taking it as fact. I'm sick of the stereotypes. I'm sick of the unwarranted hype. I'm sick of these boys being unable to demonstrate their abilities and having a coach turn a blind eye. It's transparent, and it's ugly. Nick's Junior year. A year we would all like to forget. Tryouts came, and he made varsity, which is great, as a PO. Something happened to the coach or was happening in his life, but he was a very different coach that year. He had 4, maybe five kids that he cared about. 5 out of 20 kids. Crazy right? There was no bad blood with those 4 or 5 young men; they didn't ask to be the favorites, but it was a hard season for the other 15 players. I did not witness this personally since it occurred at practice, but from other players who told their parents and then told me the coach liked to call Nick fucking fat ass. Wow. Just Wow. Nick had a very successful season on the mound. But it was not fun. It was pretty awful. Parents were writing letters to the Athletic director and everything. It was bad. High school ball was so miserable that Nick decided to play Legion Baseball. OMG so much fun. Seeing him pitch, hit, field, and run again was so nice. Knowing this would be a fun season was a giant exhale of relief. Legion was a lifesaver.

And here we are now; Senior Year has arrived. He is ready to have a great season on the mound. With a new coach and new perspective, the positive possibilities are endless. Nick's goal, and our goal, is to enjoy it. Enjoy every inning of every game. These are going to be some days to remember, and I don't want to miss a thing. Let's go, Nick!

Nick's senior year was the teams most successful season in many years. New coach with excellent experience made a big difference. Nick was a valued PO that was consistently clutch in many games. They ended up 3rd in the state and it was the best season to end his baseball career. He was happy, that made us even more happy. He has become a proud Chanticleer at Coastal Carolina, and I will always be ready to cheer for him, wherever, whenever it happens.

<u>NICK'S STATS</u>

*Stats based on the infamous Game Changer. Not all teams and stats are on this list due to not using Game Changer at the time, so all numbers are based on what we got. There were many stats to choose from, but we decided to stick to the basics.

I think it's important to recognize the hard shift in the 14U season. Pretty mind-blowing. 4 years later and I am still fucking mad..

	Plate Appear/ Batting Average	On base %/ Slugging %	Innings Pitched/ ERA:	Walks/ Strikeouts	Total chances/ Fielding %/
Energy 12U	50/.341	.420/.366	7/4.0	1/6	78/1.000
12U All stars	33/.393	.485/.536	10/ 7.7	3/11	33/.909
Energy 13U	72/.397	.520/.501	47/3.37	13/43	38/.989
Middle School	19/.375	.474/.375	10/2.10	2/11	13/.983
Energy 14U	60/.130	.333/.130	2.2/7.85	3/2	35/.943
HS/Fresh/ JV	27/.227	.320/.273	30.1/4.61	11/32	23/.913
HS/Fresh/ V	NA	NA	1/0.00	0/2	0
HS/Soph/ V	20/.211	.250/.211	29.1/3.50	9/20	12/.927
HS/ Junior/V	1/0.00	0/0	21.2/2.58	3/12	6/1.0
Legion baseball	22/.191	.259/.191	28.2/3.40	8/13	18/.889
HS/ Senior/V	NA	NA	26.1/1.595	7/23	8/1.000

<u>Overall cumulative stats:</u>

Plate Appearances/ batting average: 304/ .299
On base %/Slugging %: .391/.318
Innings pitched: 213.1
Overall ERA: 3.70
Walks: 60
K: 175
Overall Fielding %: .95%
Errors: 13

Social Media Accounts I recommend

Some of my favorite social accounts to follow, along with some of their wise words

Baseball Dudes
The reformed sports project (great podcast as well)
Coach Lisle
Dugout Confessions
Healthy Sports Parents on TikTok
Baseball and Softball Worldwide
The baseball Aholic

"Sports Parents: Instead of emphasizing the importance of your kid being the best performer on the team, emphasize the importance of being the hardest worker, best teammate, and having the best attitude on the team. Then watch the performance take care of itself."

Reformed Sport Project

"Laziness is a CHOICE. What you eat us a CHOICE. Effort is a CHOICE. Attitude is a CHOICE. Focus is a CHOICE. Energy is a CHOICE. Excuse making is a CHOICE. Accountability is a CHOICE. Routine is a CHOICE. Preparation is a CHOICE. How to respond is a CHOICE. Habits are a CHOICE. It's literally all up to you".

Baseball Dudes

"Youth Sports need a penalty box at the entrances for the attendees who can't control themselves. A public time-out so they can calm down & act like adults again"

Dugout Confessions

"On poor teams, captains lead by popularity. On great teams, captains lead by example. They arrive early, stay late, train hard, & apply the same high standards off the field"

Gary Curneen shared by Coach Lisle

"Mental Health Matters more than any stat line. Let's coach like it.

Baseball and Softball Worldwide

" A word of encouragement during a mistake is worth more than an hour of praise after success."

The Baseball Aholic

Feel Free to rip out, make copies, and throw in your pocket as a kind, gentle reminder for you and your athlete.

It is a kids' game. Breathe. Behave. Be there for your athlete. Be a cheerleader, not a dick. Focus on their goals, not yours.

It is a kids' game. Breathe. Behave. Be there for your athlete. Be a cheerleader, not a dick. Focus on their goals, not yours.

It is a kids' game. Breathe. Behave. Be there for your athlete. Be a cheerleader, not a dick. Focus on their goals, not yours.

It is a kids' game. Breathe. Behave. Be there for your athlete. Be a cheerleader, not a dick. Focus on their goals, not yours.

You love this game. This game should always be fun. Cheer on every teammate. Work hard. Respect your coach. Have so much fun, everyone will want to play the **game** with you.

You love this game. This game should always be fun. Cheer on every teammate. Work hard. Respect your coach. Have so much fun, everyone will want to play the **game** with you.

You love this game. This game should always be fun. Cheer on every teammate. Work hard. Respect your coach. Have so much fun, everyone will want to play the **game** with you.

You love this game. This game should always be fun. Cheer on every teammate. Work hard. Respect your coach. Have so much fun, everyone will want to play the **game** with you.

About the Author
JULIANNE RAMSEY

I've always loved writing, but never trained as a writer. I will forever love baseball and believe it is the greatest game in the world. I love competitiveness and passion; it can work wonders for self-confidence. I love teamwork in any area of my life. When you work together and are cooperative with each other, success is endless. Our family was handed lesson after lesson in our baseball lives. Most ended with my husband and me saying, "That can't be real". It was always real. It's hard to be in the travel world of baseball, the competitive level in any sport, for that matter. Mission accomplished if this book can make one baseball family's life even just a little easier and more rewarding. I wonder what other lessons I have learned that I will write about next.. Stay tuned.